DATA SECURITY BREACHES: CONTEXT AND INCIDENT SUMMARIES

DATA SECURITY BREACHES: CONTEXT AND INCIDENT SUMMARIES

RITA TEHAN

Novinka Books
New York

Copyright © 2008 by Nova Science Publishers, Inc.

All rights reserved. No part of this book may be reproduced, stored in a retrieval system or transmitted in any form or by any means: electronic, electrostatic, magnetic, tape, mechanical photocopying, recording or otherwise without the written permission of the Publisher.

For permission to use material from this book please contact us:
Telephone 631-231-7269; Fax 631-231-8175
Web Site: http://www.novapublishers.com

NOTICE TO THE READER

The Publisher has taken reasonable care in the preparation of this book, but makes no expressed or implied warranty of any kind and assumes no responsibility for any errors or omissions. No liability is assumed for incidental or consequential damages in connection with or arising out of information contained in this book. The Publisher shall not be liable for any special, consequential, or exemplary damages resulting, in whole or in part, from the readers' use of, or reliance upon, this material.

This publication is designed to provide accurate and authoritative information with regard to the subject matter covered herein. It is sold with the clear understanding that the Publisher is not engaged in rendering legal or any other professional services. If legal or any other expert assistance is required, the services of a competent person should be sought. FROM A DECLARATION OF PARTICIPANTS JOINTLY ADOPTED BY A COMMITTEE OF THE AMERICAN BAR ASSOCIATION AND A COMMITTEE OF PUBLISHERS.

LIBRARY OF CONGRESS CATALOGING-IN-PUBLICATION DATA
Data security breaches : context and incident summaries / Rita Tehaná, editor.
   p. cm.
   Includes bibliographical references and index.
   ISBN 978-1-60456-506-5 (softcover : alk. paper)
   1. Data protection--Law and legislation--United States. 2. Records--Access control--United States. 3. Privacy, Right of--United States. 4. Computer security--Law and legislation--United States. I. Tehan, Rita.
   KF1263.C65D35 2008
   342.7308'58--dc22
                                    2008012145

Published by Nova Science Publishers, Inc. ✢ New York

CONTENTS

Summary		1
Chapter 1	Introduction	3
Chapter 2	Statistics	7
Chapter 3	Data Security Breaches in Federal Agencies	9
Chapter 4	Data Security Breaches: Highlights	13
References		87
Index		93

SUMMARY

Personal data security breaches are being reported with increasing regularity. Within the past few years, numerous examples of data such as Social Security, bank account, credit card, and driver's license numbers, as well as medical and student records have been compromised. A major reason for the increased awareness of these security breaches is a California law that requires notice of security breaches to the affected individuals. This law, implemented in July 2003, was the first of its kind in the nation.

State data security breach notification laws require companies and other entities that have lost data to notify affected consumers. As of January 2007, 35 states have enacted legislation requiring companies or state agencies to disclose security breaches involving personal information.

Congress is considering legislation to address personal data security breaches, following a series of high-profile data security breaches at major financial services firms, data brokers (including ChoicePoint and LexisNexis), and universities. In the past three years, multiple measures have been introduced, but to date, none have been enacted.

Chapter 1

INTRODUCTION

Personal data security breaches are being reported with increasing regularity. During the past few years, there have been numerous examples of hackers breaking into corporate, government, academic, and personal computers and compromising computer systems or stealing personal data such as Social Security, bank account, credit card, and driver's license numbers, as well as medical and student records. These breaches occur not only because of illegal or fraudulent attacks by computer hackers, but often because of careless business practices, such as lost or stolen laptop computers, or the inadvertent posting of personal data on public websites. A recent infamous example occurred in May 2006, when 26.5 million veterans and their spouses were in danger of identity theft because a Veterans Affairs data analyst took home a laptop computer containing personal data (including names, Social Security numbers, and dates of birth), which was later stolen in a burglary.[1]

Depending on the definition, the most common type of identity theft is credit card fraud, and there is evidence that the extent of credit card fraud has increased due to opportunities provided by the Internet.[2] Although some aspects of identity theft have been known for many years, it is viewed now primarily as a product of the information age. A particular crime of identity theft may include one or all of these stages:

> Stage 1: Acquisition of the identity through theft, computer hacking, fraud, trickery, force, re-directing or intercepting mail, or even by legal means (e.g., purchase information on the Internet).

Stage 2: Use of the identity for financial gain (the most common motivation) or to avoid arrest or otherwise hide one's identity from law enforcement or other authorities (such as bill collectors). Crimes in this stage may include account takeover, opening of new accounts, extensive use of debit or credit cards, sale of the identity information on the street or black market, acquisition ("breeding") of additional identity related documents such as driver's licenses, passports, visas, health cards, etc.), filing tax returns for large refunds, insurance fraud, stealing rental cars, and many more.

Stage 3: Discovery of the theft. While many misuses of credit cards are discovered quickly, the "classic" identity theft involves a long period of time to discovery, typically from six months to as long as several years. Evidence suggests that the time it takes to discovery is related to the amount of loss incurred by the victim.[3]

Identity theft is rarely one crime, but is composed of the commission of a wide variety of other crimes, such as check and card fraud, financial crimes of various sorts, various telemarketing and Internet scams, auto theft, counterfeiting and forgery, etc.

The difficulty in studying identity theft is investigating what portion of the long list of identity theft related crimes is related to the "classic" type of identity theft that results in repeat victimization. For example, a common type of credit card fraud is to steal an individual's credit card. The offender makes a quick purchase of an expensive item then discards the card. Has the victim's identity truly been stolen? The event clearly fits within the definition above, but it is not the wholesale theft of the victim's identity. However, should the offender be working with an accomplice, the card could be turned over several times and even sold on the street. Finally, should the victim's driver's license and other identifying documents such as a health card with a Social Security number on it also be stolen, the basic elements for stealing an individual's identity are present.[4]

A January 2007 white paper by the computer security research company McAfee Avert Labs reports a dramatic increase in global identity theft trends.[5] One key finding was that "[p]ersonal data for tens of millions of people disappears each year. It's either been stolen or misplaced. Despite this disturbing trend, the number of complaints is surprisingly low, which leads us to believe the losses are not fully acknowledged."[6]

A California law that requires notice of security breaches to the affected individuals is the major reason for the increased awareness of these breaches.[7] This law, which was implemented in July 2003, was the first of its kind in the nation.

State security breach notification requires companies and other entities that have lost personal data to notify affected consumers. Thirty-five states have enacted legislation requiring companies or state agencies to disclose security breaches involving personal information.[8] State security freeze[9] laws allow a customer to block unauthorized third parties from obtaining one's credit report.

Chapter 2

STATISTICS

Identity theft victims spend almost 300 million hours a year trying to clear their names and re-establish good credit ratings.[10] For additional information on this topic, see CRS Report RL31919, *Remedies Available to Victims of Identity Theft*, by Gina Marie Stevens.

In December 2006, a senior editor for *Wired News* noted a milestone: "... the total number of lost or exposed personal records since February, 2005, [has passed] the 100 million mark."[11] The *New York Times* wrote an article discussing this landmark and questioned the usefulness of computing such data breaches.

> [T]he bigger picture here may be that we are now slicing and dicing the niceties of data breaches against a running tally so large, that it has lost nearly any meaning at all... 'The threat of identity theft from data losses is being greatly exaggerated,' Fred H. Cate, the director of the Center for Applied Cybersecurity Research at Indiana University in Bloomington, told this newspaper not long ago. 'And that's because a lot of people have fallen into the trap of equating data loss with identity theft.' Whether or not that is true is open to debate, but what all this data loss does represent, however, is the potential for identity theft — one that will never go away. Sure, it's a game of odds. There is only so much a crook can do with a few hundred thousand names and Social Security numbers. But once they are out there, they are out there for good. Names don't change. Neither do Social Security numbers or dates of birth. And as long as it remains easy enough to fashion that trifecta into a car loan, a home, a credit card, work papers, that would seem to be a bit of a long-term problem.[12]

The Identity Theft and Assumption Deterrence Act of 1998[13] established the Federal Trade Commission (FTC) as the government entity charged with developing "procedures to ... log and acknowledge the receipt of complaints by individuals," as well as educate and assist potential victims.[14] The FTC compiles annual reports and charts of aggregated statistics on these events, but does not identify which corporations, organizations, or other entities have been victims of security breaches. In February 2007, FTC issued its annual report on fraud complaints consumers have filed with the agency. For the seventh year in a row, identity theft topped the list, accounting for 36% of the 674,354 complaints received between January 1 and December 31, 2006.[15] Credit card fraud was the most common form of reported identity theft, followed by phone or utilities fraud, bank fraud, and employment fraud.

A number of federal agencies (e.g., the FTC, Department of Justice, Secret Service, U.S. Postal Service, and Social Security Administration), state attorneys general, and nonprofit organizations (such as the Electronic Privacy Information Center) are involved with data privacy investigations or related consumer assistance.

None of them maintain a comprehensive itemized list of data security breaches.[16] However, the Privacy Rights Clearinghouse maintains a frequently updated chronology of data breaches from February 2005 to the present.[17]

The United States Computer Emergency Readiness Team (US-CERT) interacts with federal agencies, industry, the research community, state and local governments, and others to collect reasoned and actionable cybersecurity information and to identify emerging cybersecurity threats. US-CERT has recently begun monitoring trends involving the acquisition of personally identifiable information (PII) by unauthorized, malicious users. Based on the information reported in the first quarter of FY2007, US-CERT identified the following cybersecurity trends: phishing[18] made up the bulk of security threats reported to US-CERT, accounting for almost 75% of all incidents handled. The number of reports grew by more than 500%, with just over 16,000 reports in FY2006 Q1, compared with over 103,000 in FY2007 Q1. The second highest category was "others," the bulk of which generally fell into two main areas: investigations, which were incidents found by US-CERT analysts combing through data, and incidents involving PII, both cyber and non-cyber in nature. The remaining 8% of incidents were spread across malware, equipment theft/loss, policy violations, and suspicious network activity.[19]

Chapter 3

DATA SECURITY BREACHES IN FEDERAL AGENCIES

In reports to Congress since 1997, GAO has identified information security as a government-wide high-risk issue.[20] In their FY2006 financial statement audit reports, 21 out of 24 agencies indicated that they had significant weaknesses in information security controls. As shown in reports by GAO and agency inspectors general (IG), the weaknesses persist in major categories of controls — including, for example, access controls, which ensure that only authorized individuals can read, alter, or delete data; and configuration management controls, which provide assurance that only authorized software programs are implemented. "Organizations can reduce the risks associated with intrusions and misuse if they take steps to detect and respond to incidents before significant damage occurs, analyze the causes and effects of incidents, and apply the lessons learned."[21]

In February 2007, the Federal Bureau of Investigation (FBI) reported that 160 laptop computers were lost or stolen in less than four years (February 2002 to September 2005), including at least 10 that contained sensitive or classified information — one of which held "personal identifying information on FBI personnel."[22] According to the report, the FBI failed to report 76% of the missing laptops to the Justice Department as required. [23]

A number of data security breaches by federal agencies revealed many agencies do not have adequate security controls in place[24] (see **Table 3**, below). In 2006, the list of agencies with incidents of potentially compromised data included the Departments of Agriculture, Defense, Energy, Veterans Affairs, and Transportation, the Federal Trade

Commission, the Internal Revenue Service, the Government Accountability Office, the National Institutes of Health, and the Department of the Navy. The State Department also suffered a series of hacking attacks. In FY2006, 5,146 incidents were reported to the Department of Homeland Security's incident response center for six categories of incidents, a substantial increase in the number of incidents (3,600) reported the prior year, including 706 instances of unauthorized access and 1,465 cases of malicious computer code, according to a yearly OMB report.[25]

> [E]xperts say the federal government faces special challenges because of the variety of sensitive information it keeps, the increasingly mobile nature of the federal workforce and the pervasive use of contractors, which allow thousands of individuals with varying levels of security clearance to access government databases from remote sites. A 2004 government survey on the work practices of 1.8 million federal workers found that more than 140,000 had clearance to connect with government computer systems from home. The IRS says 50,000 of its employees have laptops allowing them to access personal and business tax information from anywhere. And 133 Education Department personnel can access more than 10,000 records containing student loan recipients' personal information.[26]

In a report released in October 2006, the House Government Reform Committee[27] summarized information provided to the Committee by 19 federal departments and agencies regarding the loss or compromise of personal information since January 2003. The report finds that every agency has experienced at least one such breach and that the agencies do not always know what information has been lost or how many individuals could be affected. [28]

In June, 2006, the Office of Management and Budget issued new security guidelines requiring federal civilian agencies to implement new measures to protect sensitive personal information held by federal agencies.[29] To comply with the new policy, agencies will have to encrypt all data on laptop or handheld computers unless the data are classified as "non-sensitive" by an agency's deputy director. Agency employees also would need two-factor authentication — a password plus a physical device such as a key card — to reach a work database through a remote connection, which must be automatically severed after 30 minutes of inactivity.[30]

The President's Identity Theft Task Force,[31] which was established by Executive Order on May 10, 2006,[32] is now composed of 18 federal agencies and departments. After a year of study, the Identity Theft Task

Force released its final recommendations in April 2007.[33] The recommendations include the following:

- Reduce the unnecessary use of Social Security numbers by federal agencies,
- Establish national standards that require private sector entities to safeguard the personal data they compile and maintain and to provide notice to consumers when a breach occurs that poses a significant risk of identity theft,
- Implement a broad, sustained awareness campaign by federal agencies to educate consumers, the private sector, and the public sector on methods to deter, detect, and defend against identity theft, and
- Create a National Identity Theft Law Enforcement Center to allow law enforcement agencies to coordinate their efforts and information more efficiently, and investigate and prosecute identity thieves more effectively.[34]

In June 2006, a group of government agencies, corporations, and universities launched a research center dedicated to the study of identity fraud. The Center for Identity Management and Information Protection is dedicated to furthering a national research agenda on identity management, information sharing, and data protection.[35]

Congress considered legislation in the 109th Congress to address data security following a series of high-profile data security breaches at major financial services firms and data brokers, including ChoicePoint and LexisNexis. Multiple measures were introduced in 2005 and 2006, and several were reported out of committee, but none were brought to the floor. For information on proposed data security legislation in the 110th Congress, see CRS Report RL33273, *Data Security: Federal Legislative Approaches*, by Gina Marie Stevens.

For a discussion of legislative and other issues on this topic, see

- CRS Report RS22374, *Data Security: Federal and State Laws*, by Gina Marie Stevens;
- CRS Report RL33273, *Data Security: Federal Legislative Approaches*, by Gina Marie Stevens;
- CRS Report RS22484, *Identity Theft Laws: State Penalties and Remedies and Pending Federal Bills*, by Tara Alexandra Rainson;

- CRS Report RL33005, *Information Brokers: Federal and State Laws*, by Angie A. Welborn;
- CRS Report RL33612, *Department of Veterans Affairs: Information Security and Information Technology Management Reorganization*, by Sidath Viranga Panangala;
- CRS Report RL31919, *Remedies Available to Victims of Identity Theft* by Gina Marie Stevens; and
- CRS Report RS22082, *Identity Theft: The Internet Connection*, by Marcia S. Smith.

Chapter 4

DATA SECURITY BREACHES: HIGHLIGHTS

Tables 1 through 5 summarize selected data security or identity theft breaches reported in the press since 2000. A few highlights compiled from the report include the following.

- More than half of the security breaches occurred at institutions of higher education. (A *Chronicle of Higher Education* article examines why this is so, noting that while colleges have become better at detecting electronic break-ins, security practices, particularly password protections, are lax.[36] In addition, academic culture embraces the open exchange of information and provides a target-rich environment for data breaches — an abundance of computer equipment filled with sensitive data and a pool of financially naive students.[37]) In September 2006, Louisiana State University (LSU), under a year-long agreement with Equifax Inc., provided students, faculty and staff members with free daily monitoring of their credit reports and $2,500 in identity-theft insurance. LSU claims this is the first agreement of its kind between a credit agency and a higher-education institution. The university will pay Equifax, Inc. $150,000.[38]
- Other prevalent targets for identity theft are financial institutions (banks, credit card companies, securities companies, etc.), and government agencies (international, federal, state, and local).

- The AARP analyzed 244 publicly disclosed security breaches from January 1, 2005 through May 26, 2006, identified by the Identity Theft Resource Center (ITRC).[39] An examination of the most frequent cause of reported security breaches reveals that a third of all breaches were caused by hackers who broke into computer systems to gain access to sensitive personal information. The analysis finds that educational institutions are more likely than any other type of entity to report having had a security breach. In fact, educational institutions were more than twice as likely to report suffering a breach as any other type of entity. Physical theft of computers, computer equipment, or paper files is the next most common cause of security breaches, followed by improper display (allowing sensitive personal information to be viewed by those who should not have access (for example, printing of Social Security numbers on address labels, inadvertently making sensitive personal information accessible on Internet sites viewable by the general public, or not properly disposing of files containing sensitive personal information).

Table 1. Data Security Breaches in Businesses (2000-2007)

Business Incidents	Date Publicized	Who Was Affected	Number Affected	Type of Data Released/Compromised	Source(s)
Johnny's Selected Seeds (Winslow, ME) - hacker broke into website	March 2007	customers	11,500	credit card information **Note:** 20 stolen card numbers have been used fraudulently	"Security Log," *ComputerWorld*, March 8, 2007.
TJ Maxx date breach (see below) worse than previously thought. while the company previously believed that the intrusion took place from May 2006 to January 2007, TJX now believes its computer system was hacked in July 2005 and on various subsequent dates in 2005.	February 2007	customers	undisclosed	drivers' license numbers, names, addresses were compromised for the last four months of 2003 and May and June 2004	Greenemeir, Larry, "T.J. Maxx Probe Reveals Data Breach Worse Than Originally Thought," *Information Week*, February 21, 2007 at [http://www.informationweek.com/story/showArticle.jhtml?articleID=197007754&cid=RSSfeed_IWK_News].
KB Home - stolen computer	January 2007	customers	2,700	names, SSNs of people who had visited the sales office for Foxbank Plantation, a new home community in Berkeley County	Rupon, Kristy, "KB Home warns of ID theft risk: Home builder issues alert to customers after computer is stolen from company's Charleston sales," *The State* (Columbia, SC), January 18, 2007.

Table 1. Continued

Business Incidents	Date Publicized	Who Was Affected	Number Affected	Type of Data Released/Compromised	Source(s)
Nationwide Mutual Insurance - stolen lockbox containing customer information backup tapes stored at subcontractor Concenta Preferred Systems (Waymouth, MA) office	January 2007	customers of health insurance unit, Nationwide Health Plans	28,279	names, SSNs, hospital stay information. To find the information on the tapes requires "a very specific high-tech tape reader with matching software," that police concluded was unlikely to be accessible to the thieves	Babcock, Charles, " Data On 28,279 Nationwide Customers Stolen, *Information Week*, January 25, 2007, at [http://www.informationweek.com/story/showArticle.jhtml?articleID=197000630&cid=RSSfeed_IWK_News].
T.J. Maxx, Marshalls, HomeGoods, A.J. Wright, and possibly Bob's Stores in U.S. & Puerto Rico — Winners and HomeSense stores in Canada — and possibly T.K. Maxx stores in UK and Ireland - TJX Companies Inc. experienced an "unauthorized intrusion" into its computer systems that process and store customer transactions	January 2007	customers	undisclosed	credit card, debit card, check, and merchandise return transactions	Vijayan, Jaikumar, "Breach at TJX Puts Card Info at Risk; Network intrusion shows IT security still not up to snuff at some retailers, despite push for stronger protections," *Computerworld*, January 17, 2007.

Table 1. Continued

Business Incidents	Date Publicized	Who Was Affected	Number Affected	Type of Data Released/Compromised	Source(s)
Altria (parent company of Phillp Morris/Kraft Foods) via consultant Towers Perrin (New York, NY) - five stolen laptops	January 2007	past and present employees	18,000	names, SSNs, salaries, dates of birth **note:** employee was arrested and charged with theft	Jones, Chip. "Altria employees' data missing / Personal information was on laptop taken from firm in New York, police say," *Richmond Times-Dispatch*, January 12, 2007, p. B1.
Boeing (Seattle, WA) - laptop stolen from employee's car	December 2006	current and former employees	400,000	names, addresses, SSNs, phone numbers, dates of birth, salary information **note:** Boeing fired employee whose laptop was stolen and some managers will be disciplined	Wallace, James, "Worker Fired over Lost Laptop; Boeing Managers to Be Reprimanded for Leaving Employees Vulnerable," *Seattle Post-Intelligencer*, December 15, 2006.
Starbucks (Seattle, WA) - four laptops misplaced from headquarters	November 2006	current and former employees	60,000	names, addresses, SSNs	Harris, Craig, "Starbucks Data Missing ; Company Says Laptops with Employees' Records Are Lost," *Seattle Post-Intelligencer*, November 4, 2006, p. E1.
Gymboree (San Francisco, CA) - twice in one week, three laptops stolen from headquarters	October 2006	employees	20,000	names, SSNs	"Gymboree gumshoe hunts thief," *San Francisco Chronicle*, October 27, 2006, p. D1.

Table 1. Continued

Business Incidents	Date Publicized	Who Was Affected	Number Affected	Type of Data Released/Compromised	Source(s)
T-Mobile USA (Bellevue, WA) - laptop disappeared from employee's checked luggage (laptop was protected by password)	October 2006	current and former employees	43,000	names, addresses, SSNs, home phone numbers, dates of birth, salary information	Rogoway, Mike, "T-Mobile reports ID-theft risk," *The Oregonian (Portland)*, October 20, 2006.
General Electric (Fairfield, CT) - laptop stolen from locked hotel room (computer was password protected)	September 2006	current and former employees	50,000	names, SSNs	Anderson, Eric and Rick Clemenson, "50,000 among missing at GE ; Names in stolen laptop have retiree questioning company's need for sensitive lists," *Times-Union (Albany)*, September 27, 2006, p. A1.
AT&T - hackers broke into computer system	August 2006	customers who purchased DSL equipment from AT&T online store	19,000	credit card data	*Associated Press*, "Hackers Gain Data on AT&T Shoppers," *New YorkTimes.com*, August 30, 2006.
Automated Data Processing (ADP) (Roseland, NJ) - "an unauthorized party impersonated officers" to obtain information on investors	July 2006	individual investors with 60 companies including Fidelity, UBS, Morgan Stanley, Bear Stearns, Citigroup, Merrill Lynch	hundreds of thousands	names, addresses, number of shares held of investors	Spangler, Todd, "ADP Duped into Disclosing Data,"BaselineMag.com, July 10, 2006, at [http://www.baselinemag.com/article2/0,1540,1986655,00.asp].

Table 1. Continued

Business Incidents	Date Publicized	Who Was Affected	Number Affected	Type of Data Released/Compromised	Source(s)
Kaiser HMO - stolen laptop	July 2006	HMO subscribers to Kaiser health plan	160,000	names, phone numbers, Kaiser numbers	Singel, Ryan, "Kaiser Joins Lost Laptop Crowd," *InfoSecurity*, July 30, 2006, at [http://infosecurity.us/mambo//content/view/90/49/].
C.S. Stars (insurance contractor) - lost computer containing workers' records	July 2006	injured New York state workers (claiming compensation funds)	540,000	SSNs, names, addresses	Hines, Matt, "Insurance Company Loses 540,000 N.Y Employee Records," eWeek, July 26, 2006, at [http://www.eweek.com/article2/0,1895,1994416,00.asp].
National Association of Securities Dealers (NASD)- (Boca Raton, FL) - 10 stolen laptops	July 2006	securities dealers who were the subject of investigations involving possible misconduct.	73	SSNs of securities dealers, plus inactive account numbers of about 1,000 consumers	Jamieson, Dan, "Rule Likely on Notification of Data Breaches, Some Say; Theft of NASD Laptops Raises Questions about Regulators' security," *Investment News*, July 10, 2006, p. 2.
American Red Cross, Farmers Branch (Dallas, TX) - 3 stolen laptops	July 2006	regional blood donors	8,000	names, SSNs, birth dates, medical information	Schreier, Laura, "Donor Data Stolen at Local Red Cross Exclusive: 3 Laptops from Farmers Branch Office Held Encrypted Records," *Dallas Morning News*, July 1, 2006, p. 1A.

Table 1. Continued

Business Incidents	Date Publicized	Who Was Affected	Number Affected	Type of Data Released/Compromised	Source(s)
Bisys Group Inc.(Roseland, NJ) - employee's truck carrying backup tapes was stolen	July 2006	hedge fund donors	61,000	SSNs of 35,000 individuals	Clair, Chris, "Bisys Discloses Data Theft," *HedgeWorld Daily News*, July 6, 2006 (no page given).
American International Group (AIG)- burglary of a file server	June 2006	employees of various companies whose insurance information was submitted to AIG	970,000	names, addresses, SSNs, medical information	Smith, Elliot Blair, "AIG: Personal Data on 970,000 Lost in Burglary; Insurer Has Yet to Alert Those Affected by March 31 Break-in," *USA Today*, June 19, 2006, p. 5B.
Ernst & Young- stolen laptop	June 2006	Hotels.com customers	243,000	names, credit card numbers	Reilly, David, "Hotels.com Credit-Card Data Lost in Stolen Laptop Computer," *Wall Street Journal*, June 2, 2006, p. A14.
Union Pacific- stolen laptop	June 2006	employees of the railroad company	30,000	personal data	Vijayan, Jaikumar and Todd Weiss, "Flurry of New Data Breaches Disclosed," Computerworld, June 19, 2006 at [http://www.computerworld.com/action/article.do?command=viewArticleBasic&articleId=9001282].

Table 1. Continued

Business Incidents	Date Publicized	Who Was Affected	Number Affected	Type of Data Released/Compromised	Source(s)
Ross-Simmons- data breach	April 2006	customers	undisclosed	credit card numbers, financial information, other personal information	"Ross-Simmons Says Security Breach Exposes Customers," Computerworld, April 12, 2006, at [http://www.computerworld.com/securitytopics/security/story/0,10801,110425,00.html?source=x3888].
EBay- hackers harvesting and selling user information	March 2006	customers	undisclosed	account information	Niccolai, James, "Russian Web Site Offered eBay Account Info for $5," Computerworld, March 24, 2006, at [http://www.computerworld.com/securitytopics/security/cybercrime/story/0,10801,109881,00.html].
Deloitte & Touche- unencrypted CD left on a plane	February 2006	all U.S. and Canadian employees of McAfee Software hired before April 2005	9,200	names, SSNs, McAfee stock holdings	Kuruvila, Matthai C., "Security Giant's Data Lost," *Silicon Valley*, February 24, 2006.
Atlantis Resort- theft from the hotel's database	January 2006	customers	55,000	names, addresses, credit card details, SSNs, driver's license numbers, bank account data	"IDs of 50,000 Bahamas Resort Guests Stolen," CNet News, January 10, 2006.

Table 1. Continued

Business Incidents	Date Publicized	Who Was Affected	Number Affected	Type of Data Released/Compromised	Source(s)
Guidance Software- hacker	December 2005	security researchers and law enforcement agencies worldwide	3,800	credit card numbers	Krebs, Brian, "Hackers Break Into Computer-Security Firm's Customer Database," *Washington Post* December 19, 2005, p. D5.
Sam's Club- "card-skimming" devices	December 2005	customers who bought fuel at its gas stations between September 21 and October 2.	600	credit card information	Vijayan, Jaikumar, "Card Skimmers Eyed in Sam's Club Data Theft," Computerworld, December 14, 2005, at [http://www.computerworld.com/databasetopics/data/story/0,10801,107067,00.html].
Marriott Vacation Club International- missing data tapes	December 2005	customers and employees	206,000	addresses and credit card information	"Marriott Vacation Club reports missing data tapes," Computerworld, December 26, 2005, at [http://computerworld.com/securitytopics/security/story/0,10801,107366,00.html?SKC=security-107366].
Ford Motor Company- stolen computer	December 2005	current and former Ford employees	70,000	names and SSNs	"Tech Crime Gets Personal at Ford," CNN Money, December 22, 2005, at [http://money.cnn.com/2005/12/22/news/fortune500/ford_theft/].

Table 1. Continued

Business Incidents	Date Publicized	Who Was Affected	Number Affected	Type of Data Released/Compromised	Source(s)
Safeway - company laptop stolen from manager's home	November 2005	employees	1,200	names, SSNs, hire dates and work locations	Akkad, Dania, "Safeway Discloses Security Breach," *Monterey County Herald*, November 5, 2005 (no page given).
Boeing - theft of company computer	November 2005	current and former Boeing workers	161,000	names, Social Security numbers (SSNs), some birth dates and banking information for employees who elected to use direct deposit of payroll	Bowermaster, David and Dominic Gates and Melissa Allison, "161,000 Workers' Personal Data on PC Stolen from Boeing," *Seattle Times*, November 19, 2005, p. A1.
Eastman Kodak - laptop stolen from a consultant's locked car trunk.	June 2005	former Eastman Kodak workers	5,800	names, Social Security numbers, birth dates and benefits information	Davia, Joy, "Kodak Warns of Data Theft," *Rochester Democrat and Chronicle (New York)*, June 22, 2005, p. 8D.
Time Warner - loss of 40 computer backup tapes containing sensitive data while being shipped by Iron Mountain to an offsite storage center	May 2005	current and former employees, some of their dependents and beneficiaries, and individuals who provided services for the company	600,000	names, SSNs	Zeller, Tom, "Time Warner Says Data on Employees Is Lost," *New York Times*, May 3, 2005, p. C4.

Table 1. Continued

Business Incidents	Date Publicized	Who Was Affected	Number Affected	Type of Data Released/Compromised	Source(s)
MCI - laptop stolen from a car that was parked in the garage at the home of a MCI financial analyst	May 2005	current and former employees	16,500	names and SSNs	Young, Shawn, "MCI Reports Loss Of Employee Data On Stolen Laptop," *Wall Street Journal*, May 23, 2005, p. A2.
LEXIS/NEXIS - intruders used passwords of legitimate customers to get access to a Seisint database called Accurint, which sells reports to law-enforcement agencies and businesses. Later analysis determined that its databases had been fraudulently breached 59 times using stolen passwords.	March 2005	customers	32,000 (subsequent investigation reveals the actual number is 310,000)	names, addresses, passwords, SSNs, drivers license	El-Rashidi, Yasmine, "LexisNexis Reports Data Breach; Personal Records Are Hacked as Concerns About Security and Identity Theft Intensify," *Wall Street Journal*, March 10, 2005, p. A3; and Krim, Jonathan, "LexisNexis Data Breach Bigger Than Estimated: 310,000 Consumers May Be Affected, Firm Says," *Washington Post*, April 13, 2005, p. E1.
DSW Shoe Warehouse store - information stolen from computer database over 3-month period	March 2005	customers of 103 of the chain's 175 stores	initially "hundreds of thousands," then raised to 1.4 million	credit card information	*Associated Press*, "DSW ID Theft May Affect Over 100,000," *Chicago Tribune*, March 11, 2005, p. 4; and "Firm Raises Data Theft Count," *Washington Post*, April 19, 2005, p. E2.

Table 1. Continued

Business Incidents	Date Publicized	Who Was Affected	Number Affected	Type of Data Released/Compromised	Source(s)
T-Mobile - hacker intrusion into company database	February 2005	T-Mobile customers	400	customer records, passwords, SSNs, private e-mail and candid celebrity photos note: data offered for sale via online forum	Poulsen, Kevin, "Known Hole Aided T-Mobile Breach," Wired News, February 28, 2005, at [http://www.wired.com/news/privacy/0,1848,66735,00.html].
Motorola - Thieves broke into the offices of Affiliated Computer Services (ACS), a provider of human resources services, and stole two computers	June 2005	Motorola employees	34,000 in U.S.	SSNs and personal information	"Two Computers Stolen with Motorola Staff Data," Reuters, June 10, 2005.
ChoicePoint - criminals used fake documentation to open 50 fraudulent accounts to access consumer data	February 2005	consumers	30,000-35,000 in California; 145,000 nationwide	names, addresses, SSNs, credit reports	Perez, Evan, "ChoicePoint Is Pressed to Explain Database Breach," Wall Street Journal, February 5, 2005, p. A6.
Affiliated Computer Services - inmate hacked into county database	October 2004	county employees	900	names, birth dates, SSNs, bank account routing numbers and checking account numbers	Whaley, Monte, "FBI on Weld ID-Theft Case Feds to Analyze Data from Cell of Inmate Who Hacked Computer," Denver Post, November 11, 2004, p. B1.

Table 1. Continued

Business Incidents	Date Publicized	Who Was Affected	Number Affected	Type of Data Released/Compromised	Source(s)
Lowe's (home improvement store) - hacker used vulnerable wireless network to attempt to steal credit card info	June 2004	customers	unknown	skimmed credit card account information for every transaction processed at a particular Lowe's store	Roberts, Paul, "Wireless Hacker Pleads Guilty: Man Admits Using Store's Wireless Network to Steal Credit Card Info," PC World, June 7, 2004, at [http://msn.pcworld.com/news/article/0,aid,116411,00.asp].
eBay - hackers tricked online merchants who used the PayPal payment processing system into disclosing their user names and passwords, then logged onto the merchants' accounts	March 2004	several eBay merchants	company did not disclose	customer names, e-mail addresses, home addresses and transactions	Kirby, Carrie, "New Scam Threat at eBay / Hackers Obtained Information on Some Customers," San Francisco Chronicle, March 16, 2004, p. C1.
Kinko's - hacker installed a key logger to record every character typed on 13 Kinko's computers	November 2003	Customers at Internet terminals at 13 Kinko's copy shops in Manhattan	450	SSNs, names, passwords, credit cards, bank account data **note**: data was sold	Napoli, Lisa, "A Hacker Masters Keystroke Theft: Personal Data Stolen from 450 Victims," International Herald Tribune, August 9, 2003, p. 1.

Table 1. Continued

Business Incidents	Date Publicized	Who Was Affected	Number Affected	Type of Data Released/Compromised	Source(s)
Acxiom (marketing company) - hacker downloaded data	August 2003	clients include 14 of the top 15 credit card companies, 5 of the top 6 retail banks, IBM, Microsoft, and federal government	10% of clientele (no total number given)	passwords, personal, financial, and company information	Lee, W.A. "Hacker Breaches Acxiom Data," *American Banker*, August 11, 2003, p. 5.
DirecTV - hacker stole trade secrets for access card	April 2003	DirecTV subscribers	50,000 customers used counterfeit access cards to watch programming without paying	details about the design and architecture of DirecTV's "Period 4" cards **note**: data was sold	"U. of C. Student Pleads Guilty to Theft of Direc TV Card Data ; Trade Secrets Ended up on Hacker Site, Enabling Free Access," *Chicago Sun-Times*, April 30, 2003, p. 16.
TCI help-desk worker sold client access codes to two others, who then used the codes to obtain more than 15,000 customer credit records	November 2002	credit reporting bureau customers	15,000 (*Wired News*) 30,000 (*Seattle Times*)	names, addresses, SSNs, credit card record **note**: data sold, for $60 per	Delio, Michelle, "Cops Bust Massive ID Theft Ring," Wired News, November 25, 2002, at [http://www.wired.com/news/privacy/0,1848,56567,00.html]; and Masters, Brooke, "Huge ID-Theft Ring Broken; 30,000 Consumers at Risk ; Men Charged with Stealing Personal, Financial Data," *Seattle Times*, November 26, 2002, p. A1.

Table 1. Continued

Business Incidents	Date Publicized	Who Was Affected	Number Affected	Type of Data Released/Compromised	Source(s)
Midwest Express Airlines and Federal Aviation Administration - hackers posted list of customer names to website and posted a list of airport security screening results taken from the FAA's system	April 2002	Midwest Express Airlines customers; FAA (two separate incidents)	unknown	passenger names and airport security screening results	Larson, Virgil, "Computer Hackers Breach Midwest Express Systems," *Omaha World-Herald*, April 22, 2002, p. 1D.
ChoicePoint - Nigerian-born brother and sister posed as legitimate businesses to set up ChoicePoint accounts	2002	unknown	7,000-10,000 inquiries on names and SSNs, then used identities to commit fraud	names and SSNs **note:** data was sold	*Associated Press*, "ChoicePoint Suffered Previous Breach: Two ID Thieves Arrested in 2002 for Tapping into Data" MSNBC, February 3, 2005, at [http://www.msnbc.msn.com/id/7065902/].
New York City restaurant busboy duped credit reporting companies into providing detailed credit reports	March 2001	chief executives, celebrities and tycoons from Forbes list of richest Americans	200	SSNs, home addresses and birth dates, credit card numbers	Hays, Tom, "Busboy Hacks Only the Richest, Used Forbes' List in Plot to Steal Identity, Credit Info, Big Bucks," *Pittsburgh Post-Gazette*, March 21, 2001, p. A11.

Table 1. Continued

Business Incidents	Date Publicized	Who Was Affected	Number Affected	Type of Data Released/Compromised	Source(s)
World Economic Forum - hackers broke into computer	February 2001	attendees	3,200	passport numbers, cell phone numbers, credit card numbers, exact arrival and departure times, hotel names, room numbers, number of overnights, sessions attended, plus information on 27,000 people who have attended the global forum in recent years	Higgins, Alexander, "Hackers Steal World Leaders' Personal Data," *Chicago Sun-Times*, February 6, 2001, p. 20.
International credit card ring adds fraudulent charges of 277 Russian rubles ($5-10) to credit cards	January 2001	Internet shopping sites	unknown	credit card numbers **note:** data was sold	James, Michael, "Small-time Thefts Reap Big Net Gain Tens of Thousands of Phony $5-$10 Credit-Card Charges Rake in Millions for Hackers," *Orlando Sentinel*, January 27, 2001, p. E5.
Egghead - hacker attacked computer system	December 2000	customers	3.5 million credit card accounts; 7500 of which showed "suspected fraudulent activity"	credit card info	"Sayer, Peter, "Egghead Says Customer Data Safe After Hack Attack," PC World, January 8, 2001 at [http://msn.pcworld.com/news/article/0,aid,37781,00.asp].

Table 1. Continued

Business Incidents	Date Publicized	Who Was Affected	Number Affected	Type of Data Released/Compromised	Source(s)
Western Union - hackers made electronic copies of the credit and debit card information	September 2000	customers who transferred money on a company website	15,700	credit and debit card information	Cobb, Alan, "Hackers Steal Credit Card Info from Western Union Site," *Chicago Sun-Times*, September 11, 2000, p. 22.
America Online - AOL customer-service representatives mistakenly downloaded an e-mail attachment sent by hackers	June 2000	customers	500 records were viewed	names, addresses, and credit card numbers	"Hackers Breach Security At America Online Inc," *Wall Street Journal*, June 19, 2000, p. A34.
Two British teens intruded into 9 e-commerce websites in the United States, Canada, Thailand, Japan and Britain	March 2000	customers	26,000 credit card accounts	credit card data **note**: some data was posted on the Web	Sniffen, Michael, "2 Teens Accused of Hacking Charged in $3 Million Credit Card Theft," *Chicago Sun-Times*, March 25, 2000, p. 9.
CD Universe (online music store) - hacker stole credit card numbers and released thousands of them on a website when the company refused to pay a $100,000 ransom	January 2000	customers	300,000	credit card numbers **note**: Maxus Credit Card Pipeline Website posted up to 25,000 stolen numbers	*Associated Press*, "Hacker Said to Steal 300,000 Card Numbers," *Arizona Republic*, January 11, 2000, p. A3.

Table 1. Continued

Business Incidents	Date Publicized	Who Was Affected	Number Affected	Type of Data Released/Compromised	Source(s)
Pacific Bell - 16-year-old teenager hacked into server and stole passwords	January 2000	subscribers	63,000 accounts were decrypted; 330,000 customers told to change passwords	passwords	Gettleman, Jeffrey, "Passwords of PacBell Net Accounts Stolen; Computers: Authorities Say 16-year-old Hacker Took the Data for Fun. Theft Affects 63,000 Customers," *Los Angeles Times*, January 12, 2000, p. 2.

Table 2. Data Security Breaches in Education (2000-2007)

Education Incidents	Date Publicized	Who Was Affected	Number Affected	Type of Data Released/Compromised	Source(s)
New Mexico State Univ. (Las Cruces, NM) - personal information posted to school's website	April 2007	students	5,600	names, SSNs	Associated Press, "Personal data of NMSU students posted online," April 19, 2007.
University of California, San Francisco - computer file server stolen from locked office	April 2007	research subjects in clinical studies	3,000	names, SSNs, and for some individuals, personal health information	Rauber, Chris, "UCSF research data on at least 3,000 people missing in server theft," *San Francisco Business Times*, April 18, 2007.
Ohio State University (Columbus, OH) - two laptops stolen from professor's house in February 2007	April 2007	chemistry students	3,500	names, SSNs, employee ID numbers, birth dates, grades	Bush, Bill, "Hacker, thieves get OSU ID data: About 14,000 faculty and staff and 3,500 students affected," *Columbus Dispatch*, April 17, 2007.
Ohio State University (Columbus, OH) - hacker using foreign Internet address broke through computer firewall	April 2007	current and former staff members	17,500	names, SSNs, employee ID numbers, birth dates	Bush, Bill, "Hacker, thieves get OSU ID data: About 14,000 faculty and staff and 3,500 students affected," *Columbus Dispatch*, April 17, 2007.

Table 2. Continued

Education Incidents	Date Publicized	Who Was Affected	Number Affected	Type of Data Released/Compromised	Source(s)
Chicago Public Schools - two stolen laptops	April 2007	current and former Employees	40,000	names, SSNs	Walberg, Matthew, "Laptops with teacher data stolen," *Chicago Tribune*, April 7, 2007.
University of California, San Francisco - campus server compromised	April 2007	students, faculty, and staff associated with UCSF or UCSF Medical Center over the past two years	46,000	names, SSNs, bank accounts	Lazarus, David, "Security Breached at UCSF," *San Francisco Chronicle*, April 15, 2007, p. D1.
University of Missouri, Research Board Grant Application System (Columbia, MO) - a hacker broke into computer server	February 2007	researchers, faculty members, computer users	3,799	names, SSNs	"Hacker hits MU database: Personal info stored in computer system," *Columbia Daily Tribune* (Missouri), February 2, 2007.
Georgia Institute of Technology (Atlanta, GA) - unauthorized access to computer account	February 2007	current and former employees of School of Electrical and Computer Engineering	3,000	names, addresses, SSNs, other sensitive information	"Hackers hit Georgia Tech and steal personal info," *Atlanta Business Chronicle*, February 21, 2007.

Table 2. Continued

Education Incidents	Date Publicized	Who Was Affected	Number Affected	Type of Data Released/Compromised	Source(s)
Vanguard University (Costa Mesa, CA) - two computers stolen from financial aid office	January 2007	financial aid applicants for 2005-2006 and 2006-2007 school years	5,105	names, SSNs, dates of birth, phone numbers, driver's license numbers, lists of assets	Edds, Kimberly, "Computer theft puts financial data at risk for 5,105 students; Costa Mesa police officer says stolen equipment holds extensive information on aid applicants at Vanguard," *Orange County Register* (CA), January 27, 2007.
Eastern Illinois University (Charleston, IL) - stolen desktop	January 2007	membership rosters of of the University's 23 fraternities and sororities	1,400	SSNs, birthdates, addresses	U.S. State News, "Computer Theft Results in Security Breach; Students Notified," January 26, 2007.
University of Idaho (Moscow, ID) - theft of three desktop computers	January 2007	university alumni, donors, students and employees	70,000	names, addresses, SSNs	Prince, Brian, "University of Idaho Reports Computer Thefts," eWeek.com, January 12, 2007 at [http://www.eweek.com/article2/0,1759,2082796,00.asp?kc=EWRSS03129TX1K0000614].
Montana State University (Bozeman, MT) - student working in loan office mistakenly sent personal information to other students	December 2006	students who had paid off their student loans	259	names, SSNs	Associated Press, "University apologizes for mistakenly sharing student information," December 27, 2006.

Table 2. Continued

Education Incidents	Date Publicized	Who Was Affected	Number Affected	Type of Data Released/Compromised	Source(s)
Mississippi State University (Jackson, MS) - information inadvertently published on website	December 2006	students and employees	2,400	names, SSNs, some dates of birth	Lake, Richard, "MSU Data Put Online in Mishap," *Clarion-Ledger (Jackson, Mississippi)*, December 20, 2006, p. 1A.
University of Colorado (Boulder) - server hacked	December 2006	individuals who attended orientation sessions from 2002 to 2004	17,500	names, SSNs	Danna, Nicole, "U. Colorado security breach not used for nefarious purposes," University Wire, December 19, 2006.
Riverside High School (Durham, NC) - two students accused of hacking into databases	December 2006	employees	"thousands" (unspecified)	names, SSNs	Dopart, Brianne, "Students accused of hacking DPS; Two told teacher about security breach found during computer class," *Herald-Sun (Durham, NC)*, December 15, 2006, p. B1.
Virginia Commonwealth University (Richmond, VA) - personal information inadvertently included in two e-mail attachments	December 2006	students	561 students in the College of Humanities and Sciences	names, SSNs, addresses, grade point averages	Robertson, Gary, "E-mail includes data on students," *Richmond Times - Dispatch (Virginia)*, December 9, 2006.

Table 2. Continued

Education Incidents	Date Publicized	Who Was Affected	Number Affected	Type of Data Released/Compromised	Source(s)
University of Texas (Dallas) - computer network intrusion	December 2006	current and former students, faculty, staff, and others	5,000 - 6,000	names, SSNs, and in some cases, addresses, e-mail addresses and telephone numbers	Hacker, Holly, "UTD computer attack worse than first thought: Campus officials now say 6,000 at risk of identity theft," *Dallas Morning News*, December 14, 2006.
Nassau Community College (Garden City, NY) - theft of computer printout	December 2006	all registered students	21,000	names, addresses, SSNs, phone numbers	Winslow, Olivia, "College loses data; Printed list with personal information of Nassau Community College students gone missing, officials say," *Newsday*, December 6, 2006, p. A9.
California State University (Los Angeles) - stolen USB drive containing unencrypted personal data	November 2006	students, applicants, faculty supervisors	2,534	names, SSNs, campus identification numbers (CIN), phone numbers, e-mail addresses	US States News, "Education College Alerts Teacher Credential Applicants of Information Security Incident," November 28, 2006.
Greenville County School District (Greenville, SC) - computers containing personal information inadvertently sold at auctions	November 2006	students and employees	101,000	names, SSNs, dates of birth, addresses, phone numbers, contact information	Barnett, Ron, "Student Data Left on Sold Computers," *Greenville News (South Carolina)*, November 27, 2006, p. 1A.

Table 2. Continued

Education Incidents	Date Publicized	Who Was Affected	Number Affected	Type of Data Released/Compromised	Source(s)
Chicago Public School District - contractor mistakenly mailed personal information as part of an insurance-information package	November 2006	former school employees	1,740	names, SSNs, home addresses	Flynn, Courtney, "Teachers' IDs mailed by mistake: 1,740 Social Security numbers included in city schools' packets," *Chicago Tribune*, November 27, 2006.
Adams State College (Alamosa, CO) - stolen laptop	October 2006	high school Outward Bound students	184	unspecified personal data	Smith, Erin, "Stolen ASC laptop holds student data," *Pueblo Chieftain*, October 10, 2006.
Connors State College (Warner, OK) - stolen laptop	November 2006	students who receive Oklahoma Higher Learning Access Program scholarships	22,500	SSNs and other (unspecified) identifying information	Simpson, Susan, "Stolen computer contained student data," *Daily Oklahoman*, November 15, 2006.
University of Minnesota (Spain) - laptop stolen from a faculty member on a trip to Spain	October 2006	students	200	names, university IDs, grades	Tosto, Paul, "Second laptop with student data was stolen: No Social Security numbers compromised," *Pioneer Press (St. Paul, Minnesota)*, October 20, 2006.
University of Texas (Arlington) - stolen computers	October 2006	students	2,500	names, SSNs, university IDs, grades, emails	"U. Texas-Arlington student info on stolen computers," University Wire, October 12, 2006.

Table 2. Continued

Education Incidents	Date Publicized	Who Was Affected	Number Affected	Type of Data Released/Compromised	Source(s)
San Juan Capistrano Unified School District (CA) - theft of 5 computers	October 2006	employees	unknown	unknown	McDonald, John, "Computers stolen from offices of Capistrano school district; the five machines, valued at $5,000, may have contained confidential information on employees, a spokeswoman says," *Orange County Register (California)*, October 6, 2006, p. South_B.
Troy Athens High School (Troy, MI) - stolen hard drive	October 2006	alumni	4,400	names, addresses, SSNs	Lewis, Shawn, "Alumni will get credit watch; In wake of lost data, Troy district offers 14 months of free identity theft protection," Detroit News, October 23, 2006.
University of Iowa Department of Psychology (Iowa City, IA) - computer attack	September 2006	subjects who participated in research studies on maternal and child health from 1995 until the present.	14,500	SSNs	"University of Iowa Contacts Research Subjects about Computer Intrusion," US Fed News, September 29, 2006.

Table 2. Continued

Education Incidents	Date Publicized	Who Was Affected	Number Affected	Type of Data Released/Compromised	Source(s)
Western Illinois University - hacker accessed several electronic student services systems	July 2006	students, customers of the university's online bookstore, guests of the university hotel	180,000	SSNs, personal data, credit card information	Maguire, John, "Alums Just Told of Computer Breach: Data on 180,000 with Ties to WIU Hacked a Month Ago," *Chicago Sun-Times*, July 5, 2006, p. 8.
University of Tennessee - hacker broke into UT computer	July 2006	past and current employees	36,000	SSNs, names, addresses	Herrington, Angie, "UT Notifies Workers of Computer Hacking," *Chattanooga Times Free Press*, July 7, 2006, p. O.
Northwestern University (Chicago) - hackers broke into nine desktop computers in the Office of Admissions and Financial Aid	July 2006	students and applicants to the school	17,000	names, addresses, SSNs	"Hackers break into NU Admissions, Financial Aid Computers," *Chicago Sun Times*, July 15, 2006, at [http://www.suntimes.com/cgibin/print.cgi?getReferrer=[http://www.suntimes.com/output/news/cst-nws-hack15.html].
Moraine Park Technical College (Beaver Dam, Fond du Lac, & West Bend, WI) - missing computer disk	July 2006	apprenticeship students back to 1993	1,500	names, addresses, phone numbers, SSNs	"News Summaries Ozaukee and Washington Counties," *Milwaukee Journal Sentinel*, July 16, 2006, p. Z3.

Table 2. Continued

Education Incidents	Date Publicized	Who Was Affected	Number Affected	Type of Data Released/Compromised	Source(s)
Catawba County Schools (Newton, NC) - website exposed personal data	June 2006	students who had taken keyboarding and computer applications placement test during the 2001-02 school year	619	names, SSNs, test scores	Shain, Andrew, and Hannah Mitchell, "619 Students' Secure Data Revealed Online: Google Page Showed Social Security Numbers, Test Scores, *Charlotte Observer*, June 24, 2006, p. 1B.
San Francisco State University - faculty member's laptop stolen	June 2006	current and former students	3,000	names, SSNs, phone numbers and grade point averages.	Asimov, Nanette, "SFSU students' information stolen; School alerts 3,000 affected by theft of faculty laptop," *San Francisco Chronicle*, June 23, 2006, p. B5.
University of Kentucky- stolen thumb drive	June 2006	current and former students	6,500	SSNs	Kiernan, Vincent, "Incidents at Two Universities Put More Than 200,000 Students at Risk of Data Theft," *The Chronicle of Higher Education*, June 19, 2006, p. A21.
Ohio University (Athens, OH) - hackers breach servers in two separate incidents	May 2006	individuals and organizations listed in the alumni database, owners of patents and other intellectual property	300,00	SSNs, personal information, biographical information, patent data, intellectual property files	Vijayan, Jaikumar, "Ohio University Reports Two Separate Security Breaches," Computerworld, May 3, 2006, at [http://www.computerworld.com/action/article.do?command=viewArticleBasic&articleId=111113&intsrc=article_pots_bot].

Table 2. Continued

Education Incidents	Date Publicized	Who Was Affected	Number Affected	Type of Data Released/Compromised	Source(s)
Sacred Heart University- hackers intrude system	May 2006	students and some individuals not associated with the university	135,000	personal information, SSNs	Sandoval, Greg, "Sacred Heart is Latest University to be Hacked," CNet News, May 26, 2006, at [http://news.com.com/ 2100-7349_3-6077212.html].
University of Texas, Austin- data breach	April 2006	students, alumni, faculty, and staff of the business school	200,000	SSNs, biographical materials	*Associated Press*, "University of Texas Probes Computer Breach," MSNBC, April 24, 2006, at [http://www.msnbc.msn.com/id/12459840/].
University of Arizona- hackers break into journalism department's computer system	February 2006	journalism students	undisclosed	none so far	Grossman, Djamila, "Romanian Hacker Breaks into UA Journalism Computers," *Arizona Daily Star*, February 14, 2006, p. B2.
Notre Dame- hackers attack server	January 2006	alumni and other donors to the university	undisclosed	SSNs, credit card numbers, check images	Roberts, Paul F., "Hackers Target Notre Dame Donors," eWeek, January 24, 2006, at [http://www.eweek.com/article2/0,1895, 1915087,00.a sp].
Indiana University - malicious software programs installed on business instructor's computer	November 2005	Kelly School of Business students enrolled in introductory business course between 2001- 2005	5,300	personal student information	*Associated Press*,"IU Finds 'Malicious' Software," FortWayne.com, November 18, 2005, at [http://www.fortwayne.com/mld/fortwayne/ news/loca 1/13202338.htm].

Table 2. Continued

Education Incidents	Date Publicized	Who Was Affected	Number Affected	Type of Data Released/Compromised	Source(s)
University of Tennessee Medical Center - laptop computer stolen	November 2005	patients who received treatment in 2003	3,800	names and SSNs	"UT Patients Warned of Stolen Computer," *Chattanooga Times Free-Press*, November 2, 2005, p. B2.
Georgia Institute of Technology Office of Enrollment Services - computer theft	November 2005	past, present, and prospective students	13,000	SSNs, birth dates, names, addresses	Kantor, Arcadiy, "Georgia Tech Computer Theft Compromises Student Data," *The Technique* (via University Wire), November 11, 2005 at [http://www.nique.net/issues/2005-11-11/news/3].
University of Tennessee - inadvertent posting of names and Social Security numbers to Internet lists	October 2005	students and employees	1,900	names and SSNs	"State Briefs: UT Students' Private Data Posted on the 'Net," *The Tennessean.com*, October 29, 2005, at [http://tennessean.com/apps/pbcs.dll/article?AID=/20051029/NEWS01/510290327/1006/NEWS01].
University of Georgia - hacker hits employee records server	September 2005	current and former employees of university's College of Agricultural and Environmental Sciences	1,600	SSNs	Simmons, Kelly, "Hackers Breach Database at UGA," *The Atlanta Journal - Constitution*, September 29, 2005, p. C2.

Table 2. Continued

Education Incidents	Date Publicized	Who Was Affected	Number Affected	Type of Data Released/Compromised	Source(s)
Miami University (Ohio) - report containing SSNs and grades of more than 20,000 students has been accessible via the Internet since 2002	September 2005	students	21,762	SSNs, grades	Giordano, Joe, "Miami University, Ohio, Finds Huge Online Security Breach," *Journal-News (Hamilton, OH)*, September 16, 2005 (no page given).
Kent State University - five desktop computers stolen from campus	September 2005	students and professors	100,000	names, SSNs, grades	Gonzalez, Jennifer, "Student, Faculty Data on Stolen Computers," *Plain Dealer (Cleveland)*, September 10, 2005, p. B1.
Sonoma State University - hacking	August 2005	people who either attended, applied, graduated or worked at the school from 1995 to 2002	61,709	names, SSNs	Park, Rohnert, "Hackers Hit College Computer System: Identity Theft Fears at Sonoma State," *San Francisco Chronicle*, August 9, 2005, p. B2.
California State University - Office of the Chancellor may have experienced unauthorized access to one of its computers	August 2005	students who receive financial aid and two financial aid administrators	154	names, SSNs	"California State University Chancellor's Office Experiences Potential Computer Security Breach,"*U.S. States News*, August 29, 2005 (no page given).

Table 2. Continued

Education Incidents	Date Publicized	Who Was Affected	Number Affected	Type of Data Released/Compromised	Source(s)
University of Florida Health Sciences Center/ChartOne - stolen laptop	August 2005	patients and physicians	3,851	names, SSNs, dates of birth, medical records	Chun, Diane, "3,851 Patients at Risk of ID Theft," *Gainesville.com*, August 27, 2005 at [http://www.gainesville.com/apps/pbcs.dll/article?AID=/20050827/LOCAL/20827 0336/1078/news].
University of Colorado - hacking into campus Card Office (creates IDs for staff and students)	August 2005	students and faculty	36,000	university accounts and personal information	Uhls, Anna, "U. Colorado students getting (re)carded," *University Wire/Colorado Daily*, August 4, 2005 (no page given).
University of North Texas - hacking	August 2005	current, former and prospective students	38,607	names, addresses, telephone numbers, SSNs, student identification numbers, student ID passwords, student classification information and possibly 524 credit card numbers	Tessyman, Neal, "Hackers Steal Student Info from U. North Texas," *University Wire*, August 11, 2005 (no page given).
University of Colorado - hackers tapped into a database in the registrar's office	August 2005	student records from June 1999 to May 2001 and from fall 2003 to summer 2005.	49,000	names, SSNs, addresses, phone numbers	Mccrimmon, Katie Kerwin, "Hackers Tap CU Registrar's Database; Privacy of 49,000 Students Potentially Invaded in Breach," *Rocky Mountain News* (Denver), August 20, 2005, p. 20A.

Table 2. Continued

Education Incidents	Date Publicized	Who Was Affected	Number Affected	Type of Data Released/Compromised	Source(s)
California State University, Stanislaus - hacking	August 2005	student workers	900	names, SSNs	Togneri, Chris, "Hacker Breaks into Stan State Computer," *Modesto Bee*, August 16, 2005, p. B1.
University of Southern California - individual hacked into USC's online application system	July 2005	applicants	270,000	name, address, SSNs, e-mail address, phone number, date of birth, login information	Hawkins, Stephanie, "Hacker Hits Application System at USC," *University Wire/ Daily Trojan*, August 18, 2005 (no page given).
California Polytechnic, Pomona - two computers hacked	July 2005	university applicants and current and former faculty, staff and students	31,077	names, SSNs	Ruiz, Kenneth, "Hackers Infiltrate Cal Poly," *Whittier Daily News (CA)*, August 5, 2005 (no page given).
University of Colorado, Boulder - hackers broke into a computer server containing information used to issue identification cards	July 2005	students and professors	29,000 students and 7,000 professors	SSNs, names, photographs	*Associated Press*, "Hackers Break into CU Computers Containing 36k Records," August 1, 2005.
Michigan State University - breach of a server in the College of Education	July 2005	students	27,000	names, addresses, SSNs, course information, personal identification numbers	*Associated Press*, "Students Informed Social Security Numbers Possibly Compromised," July 7, 2005.

Table 2. Continued

Education Incidents	Date Publicized	Who Was Affected	Number Affected	Type of Data Released/Compromised	Source(s)
University of California, San Diego - hackers broke into university server	July 2005	students, staff, faculty who had attended or worked at UCSD Extension in the past five years	3,300	SSNs, driver license and credit card numbers	"SD UCSD Hackers," *City News Service*, July 1, 2005 (no page given).
California State University Dominguez Hills - hacking	July 2005	students	9613	names, SSNs	*Associated Press*, "Hackers crack computers, access private student information," July 29, 2005.
University of Connecticut - hacking - rootkit (collection of programs that a hacker uses to mask intrusion and obtain administrator-level access to a computer or computer network) placed on server on October 26, 2003, but not detected until July 20, 2005	June 2005	students, staff, and faculty	72,000	names, SSNs, dates of birth, phone numbers and addresses	Naraine, Ryan, "UConn Finds Rootkit in Hacked Server," eWeek, June 27, 2005, at [http://www.eweek.com/article2/0,1759,1831892,00.a sp].

Table 2. Continued

Education Incidents	Date Publicized	Who Was Affected	Number Affected	Type of Data Released/Compromised	Source(s)
Kent State University - laptop stolen from employee's car	June 2005	full-time faculty members since 2001	1,400	names, SSNs	Hampp, David, "Kent State U. Faculty Affected by Stolen Computer," *Daily Kent Stater* (via University Wire), June 22, 2005 (no page given).
Ohio State University Medical Center - two stolen laptops	June 2005	patients	15,000	patient names, admission and discharge dates, whether the patient had insurance, total charges and adjustments to the account.	Crane, Misti, "Laptop Containing Patients' Billing Information Stolen; Birth Dates, Social Security Numbers Not in Data Taken from Consultant, Osu Says," *Columbus Dispatch (OH)*, June 30, 2005, p. 4C.
University of Hawaii - dishonest library worker indicted on federal charges of bank fraud related to identity theft	June 2005	students, faculty, staff and library patrons at any of the 10 campuses between 1999 and 2003	150,000	SSNs, addresses and phone numbers	*Associated Press*, "UH Warns of Possible Identity Theft," June 19, 2005.
Jackson Community College (MI)- hacker breaks into computer system	May 2005	employees and students of the college	8,000	SSNs	"Computer Crime: Hacker May Have Stolen Social Security Numbers From Jackson Community Collegea," *Computer Crime Research Center*," May 29, 2005 (no page given).

Table 2. Continued

Education Incidents	Date Publicized	Who Was Affected	Number Affected	Type of Data Released/Compromised	Source(s)
Carnegie Mellon University - security breach of school's computer network	May 2005	graduates of the Tepper School of Business from 1997 to 2004; current graduate students; applicants to the doctoral program from 2003 to 2005; applicants to the MBA program from 2002 to 2004; and administrative employees	5,000	SSNs and personal information	*Associated Press*, "Carnegie Mellon Reports Computer Breach," MSNBC, April 21, 2005, at [http://msnbc.msn.com/id/7590506/].
Stanford University- computer system breach	May 2005	students and recruiters of the university	9,600	SSNs, resumes, financial data, government information	Musil, Steven, "FBI Probes Network Breach at Stanford," CNet News, May 25, 2005.
Florida International University (FIU) - a hacker acquired user names and passwords for 165 computers on campus	May 2005	faculty and students	unknown	SSNs, credit card numbers	Leyden, John, "Florida Univ on Brown Alert after Hack Attack," *The Register*, April 29, 2005, at [http://www.theregister.com/2005/04/29/fiu_id_fraud_alert/].

Table 2. Continued

Education Incidents	Date Publicized	Who Was Affected	Number Affected	Type of Data Released/Compromised	Source(s)
Northwestern University (Kellog School of Management) - computer network breach	May 2005	faculty, students, and alumni	17,500	user IDs and passwords	Meglio, Francesca Di, "Hacker Break-In," *Computer Crime Research Center*, May 23, 2005 (no page given).
University of California, San Francisco - hacker gained access to server used by accounting and personnel department	April 2005	students, faculty and staff	7,000	names and SSNs numbers	Lazarus, David, "Another Incident for UC," *San Francisco Chronicle*, April 6, 2005, p. C1.
Tufts University - possible security breach in an alumni and donor database after abnormal activity on the server in October and December, 2004	April 2005	alumni	106,000	SSNs and other unspecified personal information	Roberts, Paul, "Tufts Warns 106,000 Alumni, Donors of Security Breach: Personal Data on a Server Used for Fund Raising May Have Been Exposed," Computerworld, April 13, 2005, at [http://www.computerworld.com/securitytopics/security/privacy/story/0,10801,101043,00.html?source=x10].
University of Nevada, Las Vegas - hackers accessed school's Student and Exchange Visitor Information System (SEVIS) database	March 2005	current and former students and faculty	5,000	personal records, including birth dates, countries of origin, passport numbers, and SSNs	Lipka, Sara, "Hacker Breaks Into Database for Tracking International Students at UNLV," *Chronicle of Higher Education*, March 21, 2005, p. A43.

Table 2. Continued

Education Incidents	Date Publicized	Who Was Affected	Number Affected	Type of Data Released/Compromised	Source(s)
California State University, Chico - hackers broke into servers	March 2005	students, former students, prospective students, and faculty	59,000	SSNs	Associated Press, "Hackers Gain Personal Information of 59,000 People Affiliated with California University," *Grand Rapids Press*, March 22, 2005, p. A2.
University of California, Berkeley laptop stolen from restricted area of campus office	March 2005	alumni, graduate students, and past applicants	100,000	SSNs numbers, names; addresses, and birth dates for 1/3 of affected people	Liedtke, Michael, "Laptop Theft Causes Identity Fraud Worry," *Daily Breeze* (Torrance, CA), March 28, 2005, p. A10.
George Mason University - hackers gained access to information	January 2005	faculty, staff, and students	30,000	names, photos, SSNs, and campus ID numbers	McCullagh, Declan, "Hackers Steal ID Info from Virginia University," *Wired News*, January 10, 2005, at [http://news.com.com/2100-7349_3-5519592.html].
University of California, San Diego (UCSD) - hacker breached computer system	January 2005	students and alumni of UCSD Extension	3,500	names, SSNs	Yang, Eleanor, "Hacker Breaches Computers That Store UCSD Extension Student, Alumni Data," *San Diego Union Tribune*, January 18, 2005, p. B3.

Table 2. Continued

Education Incidents	Date Publicized	Who Was Affected	Number Affected	Type of Data Released/Compromised	Source(s)
University of California, Berkeley - hacker compromised the university's computer system	October 2004	Californians participating in California's In-Home Supportive Services program since 2001	1.4 million individuals	SSNs, names, addresses, phone numbers, and dates of birth	Reuters, "Hacker Strikes University Computer System," CNET News, October 19, 2004, at [http://news.com.com/2100-7349_3-5418388.html].
California State - auditor from chancellor's office lost hard drive containing personal information	August 2004	380,000 current and former students, applicants, staff, faculty and alumni at UC San Diego and 178,000 at San Diego State	23,500	name, address, SSNs	Connell, Sally Ann, "Security Lapses, Lost Equipment Expose Students to Possible ID Theft; in the Latest Incident, a Cal State Hard Drive with Data on 23,500 Individuals Is Missing," *Los Angeles Times*, August 29, 2004, p. B4.
University of California, Los Angeles - stolen laptop w/ blood donor info	June 2004	blood donors	145,000	names, birth dates and SSNs	Becker, David, "UCLA Laptop Theft Exposes ID Info," CNET News, October 6, 2004, at [http://news.com.com/UCLA+laptop+theft+exposes+ID+info/2100-1029_3-5230662.html?tag=nl].

Table 2. Continued

Education Incidents	Date Publicized	Who Was Affected	Number Affected	Type of Data Released/Compromised	Source(s)
University of California, San Diego (UCSD) - hackers breached security at the San Diego Supercomputer Center and the University's Business and Financial Services Department	April 2004	UCSD students, alumni, faculty, employees and applicants	380,000	SSNs, and driver license numbers	Sidener, Jonathan, "SD Supercomputer Center Among Victims of Intrusion," *San Diego Union Tribune*, April 15, 2004, p. B3.
Georgia Institute of Technology	March 2003	patrons of art and theatre program	57,000	credit card numbers	Lemos, Robert, "Data Thieves Strike Georgia Tech," Wired News, March 31, 2003, at [http://news.com.com/Data+thieves+strike+Georgia+Tech/2100-1002_3-994821.html?tag=nl].
University of Texas, Austin - computer hackers broke into database on multiple occasions	March 2003	current and former student, faculty and staff members, as well as job applicants	55,200	names, addresses, SSNs, email addresses, office phone numbers **note:** perpetrator claimed he did not distribute the numbers and had not used them "to anyone's detriment"	Read, Brock, "Hackers Steal Data From U. of Texas Database," *Chronicle of Higher Education*, March 21, 2003, p. 35.

Table 2. Continued

Education Incidents	Date Publicized	Who Was Affected	Number Affected	Type of Data Released/Compromised	Source(s)
University of Kansas - hacker break-in to Student and Exchange Visitor Information System (SEVIS)	January 2003	foreign students	1,400	SSNs, passport numbers, countries of origin, and birth dates.	Arnone, Michael, "Hacker Steals Personal Data on Foreign Students at U. of Kansas,"*Chronicle of Higher Education*, January 24, 2003 (no page given).
College of the Canyons (California) - computer hard drive containing personal student information stolen	October 2001	current and former students	36,000	names, SSNs, and photographs	Mistry, Bhavna, "Identity Theft Alert Issued at College," *Los Angeles Daily News*, October 21, 2001, p. N7.
University of Washington Medical Center - hacker broke into computer system	December 2000	cardiology and rehabilitation patients	5,000	names, addresses, birth dates, heights and weights, SSNs, and the medical procedure undergone	"Hacker Steals Patient Records," *San Diego Union-Tribune*, December 9, 2000, p. A3.

Table 3. Data Security Breaches in Financial Institutions (2001-2007)

Financial Institutions Incidents	Date Publicized	Who Was Affected	Number Affected	Type of Data Released/Compromised	Source(s)
New Horizons Community Credit Union (Denver, CO) - stolen laptop. Note: computer was protected by two layers of security, a unique user-identifier, and a multiple-character, alpha-numeric password.	April 2007	credit union members	9,000	loan account information	States News Service, "New Horizons Community CU Takes Action after Potential Data Breach; Members Informed of Protections," April 11, 2007.
MoneyGram International - server unlawfully accessed	January 2007	customers	79,000	names, addresses, phone numbers, and in some cases, bank accounts	Onaran, Yalman and Elizabeth Hester, "Breach affects 79,000 MoneyGram accounts; Money-transfer and bill-paying service doesn't know if hackers stole personal data," *Saint Paul Pioneer Press (Minnesota)*, January 13, 2007, p. 1C.
Premier Bank - report stolen from truck	December 2006	customers	1,8000	names, account numbers of customers who opened accounts in October, 2006	Sorkin, Michael, " Bank data stolen out of exec's vehicle: Names with account numbers were in truck outside award ceremony," *St. Louis Post-Dispatch*, December 6, 2006, p. C1.

Table 3. Continued

Financial Institutions Incidents	Date Publicized	Who Was Affected	Number Affected	Type of Data Released/Compromised	Source(s)
TD Ameritrade - criminals, using stolen customer accounts acquired from a hacked computer, drove up the prices of low-priced stocks through high-volume purchases and then sold those shares at a profit	December 2006	customers	unknown; company has 6 million clients	names, addresses, birth dates, SSNs **note:** TD Ameritrade had to cover $4 million in fraudulent transactions for its most recent quarter	Greenemeier, Larry, "Cybercrooks Get Smarter; E-Trade and TD Ameritrade were victims of an online brokerage pump-and-dump scheme," *Wall Street & Technology*, December 1, 2006, p. 14.
ING Financial Services- stolen laptop	June 2006	District of Columbia government workers and retirees	13,000	SSNs, personal data	Dwyer, Timothy, "ING Financial to Notify Potential Identity Theft Victims," *Washington Post*, June 19, 2006, p. B4.
Equifax Inc.- stolen laptop	June 2006	nearly all the U.S. employees of the credit reporting bureau	2,500	names, SSNs	Stempel, Jonathan, "Equifax Says Laptop With Employee Data Was Stolen," eWeek, June 20, 2006, at [http://www.eweek.com/article2/0,1759,1979296,00.asp?kc=EWRSS03129TX1K0000614].

Table 3. Continued

Financial Institutions Incidents	Date Publicized	Who Was Affected	Number Affected	Type of Data Released/Compromised	Source(s)
Fidelity Investments- stolen laptop	March 2006	Hewlett-Packard employees	196,000	personal data	Hines, Matt, "Stolen Fidelity Laptop Exposes HP Workers," eWeek, March 23, 2006, at [http://www.eweek.com/article2/0,1895,1942049,00.asp].
Bank of America, Washington Mutual- debit cards cancelled	February 2006	customers using debit cards issued by the two banks at Sam's Club gas stations and Office Max	200,000	debit card information which was used to accrue fraudulent charges	Sandoval, Greg "Web of Intrigue Widens in Debit-Card Theft Case," CNet News, February 13, 2006, at [http://news.com/Web+of+intrigue+widens+in+debitcard+theft+case/2100-1 029_3-6038405.html].
Ameriprise Financial- laptop theft	January 2006	customers and advisers with the financial firm	230,000	names, SSNs, internal account numbers	Dash, Eric, "Ameriprise Loses Data on 230,000 Customers and Advisers," *New York Times*, January 25, 2006.
H&R Block- Social Security numbers printed on unsolicited packages containing free software	January 2006	recipients of the company's tax preparation software	undisclosed	SSNs	Gilbert, Alorie, "H&R Block Blunder Exposes Consumer Data," CNet News, January 3, 2006, at [http://news.com/H38R+Block+blunder+exposes+consumer+data/2100-102 9_3-6016720.html].

Table 3. Continued

Financial Institutions Incidents	Date Publicized	Who Was Affected	Number Affected	Type of Data Released/Compromised	Source(s)
Visa USA	December 2005	customers with Visa cards from various financial institutions using a mutual merchant	undisclosed	credit card information	Weinstein, Natalie, "Visa Deals With Possible Data Breach," CNet News, December 24, 2005, at [http://news.com.com/2100-1029_3-6007759.html].
Scottrade Inc.- internet hacker	December 2005	customers of the stock brokerage firm	140,000	names, birth dates, drivers license numbers, phone numbers, bank names, bank routing numbers, bank account numbers, and Scottrade account numbers	"Hackers Reveal 140,000 Customer ID's," *Computer Crime Research Center*, December 2, 2005 (no page given).
TransUnion (credit reporting bureau) - stolen desktop computer	November 2005	customers	3,600	SSNs and personal credit information	Paul, Peralte, "Credit Bureau Burglary Leaves 3,600 Vulnerable," *Atlanta Journal and Constitution*, November 11, 2005, p. 5G.
Choicepoint - Miami-Dade County Police Department may have misused the department's account to illegally access consumer records	September 2005	consumers	5,103	SSNs, driver's license information	Husted, Bill, "Another Breach of Records Feared; Choicepoint Tells 5,103 Customers about Incident," *Atlanta Journal-Constitution*, September 17, 2005, p. 1H.

Table 3. Continued

Financial Institutions Incidents	Date Publicized	Who Was Affected	Number Affected	Type of Data Released/Compromised	Source(s)
Bank of America - stolen laptop	September 2005	Visa Buxx card users	undisclosed	names, credit card numbers, bank account numbers, routing transit numbers	McMillan, Robert, "Bank of America Notifying Customers After Laptop Theft," Computerworld, October 7, 2005, at [http://www.computerworld.com/securitytopics/security/story/0,10801,105246,00.html].
J.P. Morgan (Dallas) - stolen laptop	August 2005	clients	unknown	personal and financial information	"Security Breach at J.P. Morgan Private Bank," *AFX International Focus*, August 30, 2005 (no page given).
Citigroup - a box of computer tapes with account information for 3.9 million customers was lost in shipment by CitiFinancial, a unit of Citigroup	June 2005	personal and home equity loan customers	3.9 million	names, addresses, SSNs and loan-account data	Krim, Jonathan, "Customer Data Lost, Citigroup Unit Says:3.9 Million Affected As Firms' Security Lapses Add Up, *Washington Post*, June 7, 2005, p. A1.
Japanese credit cardholders - hackers behind U.S. data theft may have compromised the data of Japanese cardholders, according to the government. Fraudulent transactions have now emerged in Japan.	June 2005	customers of 26 domestic Japanese credit card firms	unknown	unknown	"Japan Cardholders 'Hit' by Theft," *BBC News*, June 21, 2005 at [http://news.bbc.co.uk/2/hi/business/4114252.stm].

Table 3. Continued

Financial Institutions Incidents	Date Publicized	Who Was Affected	Number Affected	Type of Data Released/Compromised	Source(s)
MasterCard - breach occurred in 2004 at a processing center in Tucson operated by CardSystems Solutions, one of several companies that handle transfers of payment between the bank of a credit card-using consumer and the bank of the merchant where a purchase was made. CardSystems' computers were breached by malicious code that allowed access to customer data.	June 2005	MasterCard credit card and some debit card customers	40 million	names, account numbers, security codes, expiration dates	Krim, Jonathan and Michael Barbaro, "40 Million Credit Card Numbers Hacked: Data Breached at Processing Center,"*Washington Post*, June 18, 2005, p. A1; Zeller, Tom and Eric Dash, "MasterCard Says 40 Million Files Put at Risk,"*New York Times*, June 18, 2005, p. A1; and Evers, Joris, "Credit Card Suit Now Seeks Damages," CNET News.com, July 7, 2005, at [http://news.com.com/Credit+card+suit+now+seeks+damages/2100-7350_3-5777 818.html].
Bank of America - laptop stolen from car in Walnut Creek, CA	June 2005	California customers	18,000	names, addresses, SSNs,	Lazarus, David, "Breaches in Security Require New Laws," *San Francisco Chronicle*, June 29, 2005, p. C1.

Table 3. Continued

Financial Institutions Incidents	Date Publicized	Who Was Affected	Number Affected	Type of Data Released/Compromised	Source(s)
New Jersey cybercrime ring stole financial records from bank accounts	May 2005	customers of four banks (Charlotte, North Carolina-based Bank of America and Wachovia, Cherry Hill, New Jersey-based Commerce Bank, and PNC Bank of Pittsburgh)	700,000	names, SSNs, bank account information **note:** bank employees sold financial records to collection agencies and law firms.	Weiss, Todd, "Scope of Bank Data Theft Grows to 676,000 Customers: Bank Employees Used Computer Screen Captures to Snag Customer Data," Computerworld, May 20, 2005, at [http://www.computerworld.com/securitytopics/security/cybercrime/story/0,10801,101903,00.html].
Ameritrade (securities broker) - loses tapes with back-up information on customer accounts	April 2005	Ameritrade current and former customers	200,000	account information	"Ameritrade Loses Customer Account Info," CNN Money, April 19, 2005, at [http://money.cnn.com/2005/04/19/technology/ameritrade/index.html].
HSBC (global bank) sent out warning letters notifying customers that criminals may have gained access to credit card info	April 2005	holders of General Motors MasterCard who had shopped at Polo Ralph Lauren stores	180,000	credit card information	"Security Scare Hits HSBC's Cards," BBC News, April 14, 2005, at [http://news.bbc.co.uk/2/hi/business/444477.stm]; and Vijayan, Jaikumar, "Update: Scope of Credit Card Security Breach Expands," Computerworld, April 15, 2005, at [http://www.computerworld.com/securitytopics/security/story/0,10801,101101,0 0.html].

Table 3. Continued

Financial Institutions Incidents	Date Publicized	Who Was Affected	Number Affected	Type of Data Released/Compromised	Source(s)
Bank of America - computer data tapes lost during shipment	February 2005	GSA charge card program (Visa cards issued to federal employees)	1.2 million	customer and account information	Cairns, Ann, "Bank of America Is Missing Tapes With Card Data,"*Wall Street Journal*, February 28, 2005, p. B2.
Wells Fargo - computers stolen from Wells Fargo vendor	November 2004	mortgage and student-loan customers	company would not disclose	customers' names, addresses, and SSNs, and account numbers	Breyer, R. Michelle, "Wells Fargo Customer Data Stolen in Computer Theft,"*Austin-American Statesman*, November 3, 2004, p. D1.
Wells Fargo - hacker arrested with stolen computers and laptop	November 2003	customers with personal lines of credit used for consumer loans and overdraft protection	company would not disclose	names, addresses, account and SSNs	"Suspect Is Arrested in Theft of Bank Data," *Los Angeles Times*, November 27, 2003, p. C2.
Weichert Financial Services - credit profiles were unlawfully accessed from internal computer system	May 2003	clients	3,774	credit reports, driver's license info	*Associated Press*, "Pair Accused of Fraud in Credit Reports' Theft: Allegedly Used Data to Buy Goods over the Internet,"*The Record* (Bergen County, NJ), May 2, 2003, p. A10.

Table 3. Continued

Financial Institutions Incidents	Date Publicized	Who Was Affected	Number Affected	Type of Data Released/Compromised	Source(s)
Visa, MasterCard, American Express and Discover account numbers - hacker stole 8 million	February 2003	credit card customers	PNC Bank cancelled 16,000 cards; Citizens Bank cancelled 8,000-10,000 cards	ATM/debit/check cards	Sabatini, Patricia, "PNC Cancels 16,000 Cards After Hacking Theft Incident," *Pittsburgh Post-Gazette*, February 20, 2003, p. C1.
Fullerton, California - bogus credit card ring opened bank accounts, credit lines, auto and home loans	June 2001	impersonated more than 1,500 people nationwide and defrauded 76 financial institutions	1,500	birth dates, SSNs, mothers' maiden names, credit cards, driver's licenses, and receipts for car and home purchases.	Brown, Aldrin and Jeff Collins, "Suspicious Mail Triggered Probe of Identity Theft Crime Losses from the Alleged Ring, Which Used Data Stolen as Far Back as the Early '90s, May Hit $10 Million," *Orange County Register*, June 21, 2001 (no page given).

Table 4. Data Security Breaches in Local, State, and Federal Government (2003-2007)

Government (Local, State and Federal) Incidents	Date Publicized	Who Was Affected	Number Affected	Type of Data Released/Compromised	Source(s)
Transportation Security Administration - missing external hard drive	May 2007	individuals employed by the agency from January 2002 until August 2005	100,000	name, SSN, date of birth, payroll information, bank account and routing information	Hu, Spencer, "TSA Hard Drive With Employee Data Is Reported Stolen," *Washington Post*, May 5, 2007, p. A9.
U.S. Department of Agriculture - public information disclosed for more than a decade on public website	April 2007	recipients of loans or other financial assistance	63,000 (first estimate), then 38,700 (after USDA investigation)	SSNs	Nakashima, Ellen, "U.S. Exposed Personal Data; Census Bureau Posted 63,000 Social Security Numbers Online," *Washington Post*, April 2, 2007, p. A5 and Prince, Brian, "USDA Cuts Number Affected by Data Exposure," *eWeek*, April 23, 2007.
Georgia Secretary of State (Atlanta, GA) - 30 boxes of voter registration records found in trash	April 2007	Fulton County voters	75,000	name, address, SSNs	Associated Press, "75,000 voter registration cards found in trash bin in Atlanta," April 12, 2007.
ChildNet (non-profit that runs Broward County's child welfare program (Fort Lauderdale, FL) - former employee allegedly stole laptop	April 2007	adoptive and foster-care parents	12,000	SSNs, financial and credit data, driver's license data, passport numbers	Haas, Brian, and Bill Hirschman, "Stolen ChildNet laptop puts 12,000 at risk of ID theft," *South Florida Sun-Sentinel* (Fort Lauderdale), April 12, 2007.

Table 4. Continued

Government (Local, State and Federal) Incidents	Date Publicized	Who Was Affected	Number Affected	Type of Data Released/Compromised	Source(s)
Los Angeles County Child Support Services (Los Angeles, CA) - three missing laptops	March 2007	child support clients	243,000	130,500 SSNs (most without names attached), about 12,000 individuals' names and addresses, and more than 101,000 child support case numbers	Rosenblatt, Susannah, "Child support data may be at risk; L.A. County agency tells 243,000 clients that three missing laptops may contain personal info," *Los Angeles Times*, March 30, 2007, p. B4.
Fort Monroe (Fort Monroe, VA) - stolen Army laptop	March 2007	civilian employees	16,000	names, SSNs, payroll information	Howe, Kevin, "Army warns of data theft: laptop with information of 16,000 civilian employees stolen in Virginia," *Monterey County Herald* (California), March 29, 2007.
California National Guard (Sacramento, CA) - stolen computer hard drive	March 2007	California National Guard troops deployed to the U.S.-Mexico border	1,300	names, addresses, SSNs, dates of birth	Associated Press, "Stolen hard drive contains data for California Guard troops," March 10, 2007.
U.S. Department of Veterans Affairs, VA Medical Center (Birmingham, AL) - missing hard drive	February 2007	veterans	535,000. Hard drive also may have included data, not all of it sensitive, on about 1.3 million non-VA physicians, both living and dead	names, SSNs, some Medicare billing record information and billing codes for 1.3 million doctors	Thornton, William, "535,000 on lost VA drive: Agency to notify those possibly affected," *Birmingham News* (Alabama), February 12, 2007.

Table 4. Continued

Government (Local, State and Federal) Incidents	Date Publicized	Who Was Affected	Number Affected	Type of Data Released/Compromised	Source(s)
Connecticut - personal information inadvertently posted to state Administrative Services Department's website	February 2007	state employees	1,700	names, SSNs	Greenemeir, Larry, "Stop & Shop PIN Pads Breached; Connecticut Removes Worker Data From Site," *Information Week*, February 20, 2007, at [http://www.informationweek.com/story/showArticle.jhtml?articleID=197007473&cid=RSSfeed_IWK_News]
Massachusetts Department of Industrial Accidents (Boston, MA) - contractor accessed a workers' compensation data file and stole the identities of at least three people, opened credit card accounts in their names, and charged thousands of dollars for jewelry and other purchases	February 2007	accident victims	1,200	names, SSNs	Murphy, Sean, "Worker charged with identity theft," *Boston Globe*, February 2, 2007.
Chicago Board of Elections - computer disks mistakenly distributed to aldermen and ward committeemen	January 2007	Chicago voters	1.3 million	names, SSNs, dates of birth, addresses	Associated Press, Social Security numbers distributed on computer discs," January 23, 2007.
Note: class-action lawsuit was filed against the Board of Elections in Cook County Circuit Court					

Table 4. Continued

Government (Local, State and Federal) Incidents	Date Publicized	Who Was Affected	Number Affected	Type of Data Released/Compromised	Source(s)
Internal Revenue Service, Kansas City, KS - 26 computer tapes missing **Note**: tapes require special equipment to read and software that is not commonly used	January 2007	taxpayers	unknown	unknown (potentially contain taxpayers' names, SSNs, bank account numbers, or employer information)	Horsley, Lynne, "26 IRS tapes missing from City Hall: Records were delivered from City Hall in August. Trail of where taxpayer data went is under investigation," *Kansas City Star*, January 19, 2007, p. A1.
Indiana State Department of Health via Family Health Center of Clark County (Jeffersonville, IN) - two stolen computers	November 2006	women in the state's Breast and Cervical Cancer Program	7,700	name, address, SSN, medical information	Associated Press, "Women alerted to possible identity theft," November 26, 2006.
Bowling Green Police Dept. (Bowling Green, OH) - inadvertent publishing of personal data to website	November 2006	victims or suspects on the daily blotter	200	names, SSNs, phone numbers	Feehan, Jennifer, "Bowling Green police mistakenly put private data online," *Blade (Toledo, Ohio)*, November 14, 2006.
Administration for Children's Services (New York, NY) - unshredded files found on the street in clear plastic garbage bag	November 2006	families, social workers and police	200 case files	unspecified confidential information	Schapiro, Rich and Nicole Bode, "Secret Shame for All to See. Confidential Acs Files Found Dumped on Street," *New York Daily News*, November 20, 2006, p. 3.

Table 4. Continued

Government (Local, State and Federal) Incidents	Date Publicized	Who Was Affected	Number Affected	Type of Data Released/Compromised	Source(s)
City of Lubbock (TX) - hackers broke into city job application website	November 2006	job applicants	5,800	names, addresses, SSNs, drivers license numbers	Roberts, Paul, "Texas Tech-are police discover security breach in city database" (sic), University Wire, November 9, 2006.
Manhattan Veterans Affairs Medical Center, New York Harbor Health Care System (New York, NY) - unencrypted stolen laptop	November 2006	veterans who receive pulmonary care at the facility	1,600	names, SSNs, medical diagnoses	Hutchinson, Bill, "Your Identity May Be Stolen, Vets Are Warned, *New York Daily News*, November 2, 2006, p. 19.
Veterans Affairs Hospital and McAlester Clinic - missing computer disks (Muskogee, OK)	November 2006	veterans	1,400	names, SSNs, billing information	Thornton, Tony, "VA hospital loses data on patients; No indication of misuse, agency says," *The Oklahoman*, November 2, 2006, p. 1A.
U.S. Army Cadet Command (Fort Monroe, VA) - stolen laptop	November 2006	high school students who applied for Army ROTC scholarships.	4,600	names, addresses, W-2 tax forms, SSNs	Petkofsy, Andrew, "ROTC applicants' data on stolen computer," *Richmond Times Dispatch (Virginia)*, November 2, 2006, p. B6.
Colorado Dept. of Human Services via private contractor Affiliated Computer Services (Dallas, TX) - stolen computer	November 2006	recently hired employees	up to 1.4 million	names, SSNs, birth dates	Migoya, David, "Stolen state database puts 1.4 million at ID-theft risk," *Denver Post*, November 2, 2006, p. B1.

Table 4. Continued

Government (Local, State and Federal) Incidents	Date Publicized	Who Was Affected	Number Affected	Type of Data Released/Compromised	Source(s)
Port of Seattle (Seattle, WA) - missing CD-ROMS	October 2006	individuals who applied for airport security badges	6,943	unspecified personal information	"Port of Seattle Hires Id Protection Service," *Pacific Shipper*, October 27, 2006.
Camp Pendleton Marine Corps base, via Lincoln BP Management (near Oceanside, CA) - missing laptop	October 2006	Marines who live on the base	2,400	unspecified personal information	Hoellworth, John, "Lost laptop contains 2,400 Pendleton Marines' info," *Marine Corps Times*, October 23, 2006, p. 13.
City of Visalia, Recreation Division (Visalia, CA) - city documents were found scattered on a city street.	October 2006	current and former employees	200	names, SSNs	Castellon, David, "Tossed records are still a mystery," *Visalia Times-Delta (California)*, October 17, 2006, p. 1C.
Poulsbo Department of Licensing (Poulsbo, WA) - missing data backup device	October 2006	citizens processed at one workstation	2,200	names, addresses, drivers license photos	US States News, "Small Department of Licensing Data Backup Device Missing," October 10, 2006.
Congressional Budget Office - mailing list hacked and phishing email that appeared to come from CBO was sent	October 2006	subscribers to CBO's mailing list	unknown	unknown	"Hackers Breach Budget Office's Mailing List," *National Journal*, *Technology Daily*, October 13, 2006.

Table 4. Continued

Government (Local, State and Federal) Incidents	Date Publicized	Who Was Affected	Number Affected	Type of Data Released/Compromised	Source(s)
Cleveland Air Route Traffic Control Center (Oberlin, OH) - computer hard drive stolen	October 2006	air traffic controllers	400	names, SSNs	Sangiacomo, Michael, "FAA data in Oberlin computer lost Drives had names, Social Security numbers," *Cleveland Plain Dealer*, October 6, 2006, p. B3.
Florida Department of Labor - personal information inadvertently posted on test server	October 2006	individuals enrolled for services with regional workforce boards	4,624	names, SSNs,	Samples, Eve, "More than 4,600 Floridians' personal data accidentally posted,"*Palm Beach Post*, October 11, 2006.
Cumberland County, PA - SSNs in meeting minutes posted on website	October 2006	employees	1,200	names, SSNs	Miller, Matt, "Employee numbers removed from Web," *Patriot-News*, October 3, 2006, p. B1.
Poulsbo Department of Licensing (Poulsbo, WA) - missing data backup device	October 2006	citizens processed at one workstation	2,200	names, addresses, drivers license photos	US States News, "Small Department of Licensing Data Backup Device Missing," October 10, 2006.
Congressional Budget Office - mailing list hacked and phishing email that appeared to come from CBO was sent	October 2006	subscribers to CBO's mailing list	unknown	unknown	"Hackers Breach Budget Office's Mailing List," *National Journal, Technology Daily*, October 13, 2006.

Table 4. Continued

Government (Local, State and Federal) Incidents	Date Publicized	Who Was Affected	Number Affected	Type of Data Released/Compromised	Source(s)
Cleveland Air Route Traffic Control Center (Oberlin, OH) - computer hard drive stolen	October 2006	air traffic controllers	400	names, SSNs	Sangiacomo, Michael, "FAA data in Oberlin computer lost Drives had names, Social Security numbers," *Cleveland Plain Dealer*, October 6, 2006, p. B3.
Florida Department of Labor - personal information inadvertently posted on test server	October 2006	individuals enrolled for services with regional workforce boards	4,624	names, SSNs,	Samples, Eve, "More than 4,600 Floridians' personal data accidentally posted," *Palm Beach Post*, October 11, 2006.
Cumberland County, PA - SSNs in meeting minutes posted on website	October 2006	employees	1,200	names, SSNs	Miller, Matt, "Employee numbers removed from Web," *Patriot-News*, October 3, 2006, p. B1.
Kentucky Personnel Cabinet (Frankfort, KY) - letters sent to employees displayed their SSNs on front	September 2006	employees in state agencies, community and technical colleges, school districts, health departments and other offices covered by the state's insurance program	146,000	SSNs	Alford, Roger, "State sends out letters with Social Security numbers visible," Associated Press, September 29, 2006.

Table 4. Continued

Government (Local, State and Federal) Incidents	Date Publicized	Who Was Affected	Number Affected	Type of Data Released/Compromised	Source(s)
North Carolina Department of Motor Vehicles (Louisburg, NC) - stolen computer	September 2006	drivers	16,000	names, SSNs, driver's license numbers, dates of birth	"Thieves take N.C. DMV computer with personal info," Associated Press, September 28, 2006.
U.S. Department of Commerce - 1,137 stolen, lost, or missing laptops	September 2006	Census Bureau and National Oceanic and Atmospheric Administration	6,200 households (estimated)	unknown	Sipress, Alan, "1,100 Laptops Missing from Commerce Dept.," *Washington Post*, September 22, 2006, p. A3.
U.S. Department of Veterans Affairs - missing computer from contractor's office	August 2006	patients at VA hospitals in Pennsylvania	38,000	SSNs, names, addresses, birth dates, insurance carriers, billing information, details of service	Rash, Wayne, "Another VA Computer Goes Missing," *eWeek*, August 7, 2006, at [http://www.eweek.com/article2/0,1895,2000268,00.asp].
U.S. Department of Transportation - stolen laptop	August 2006	drivers license records of Florida residents	133,000	SSNs, names, addresses	Rash, Wayne, "DOT is the Latest Victim of Computer Theft," *eWeek*, August 10, 2006, at [http://www.eweek.com/article2/0,1895,2002148,00.asp?kc=EWNAVEMNL081106EOAD].

Table 4. Continued

Government (Local, State and Federal) Incidents	Date Publicized	Who Was Affected	Number Affected	Type of Data Released/Compromised	Source(s)
U.S. Department of Education - exposed loan data	August 2006	students who borrowed money under the Federal Direct Student Loan program	21,000	names, birth dates, SSNs, addresses, phone numbers and in some cases account information for holders of federal direct student loans	Yen, Hope, "Ed. Dept. offers free credit monitoring," *Houston Chronicle*, August 24, 2006 (no page given).
Naval Safety Center - personal data exposed on website and on 1,100 computer discs mailed to naval commands	July 2006	Naval and Marine Corps aviators and air crew, both active and reserve	"more than 100,000"	SSNs, personal information	"Naval Safety Center Finds Personal Data on Website," U.S. Department of Defense press release, July 8, 2006, at [http://www.news.navy.mil/search/display.asp?s tory_id=24568].
U.S. State Department - hackers	July 2006	Washington headquarters, and the Bureau of East Asian and Pacific Affairs	unknown	access to data and passwords	"State Department Releases Details Of Computer System Attacks," *COMMWEB*, July 13, 2006 (no page given), and Greenemeier, Larry, "State Department Hack Escalates Federal Data Insecurity," Information Week, July 12, 2006, at [http://www.informationweek.com/news/showArticle.jhtml?articleID=190302905].

Table 4. Continued

Government (Local, State and Federal) Incidents	Date Publicized	Who Was Affected	Number Affected	Type of Data Released/Compromised	Source(s)
U.S. Department of Transportation - stolen laptop	August 2006	drivers license records of Florida residents	133,000	SSNs, names, addresses	Rash, Wayne, "DOT is the Latest Victim of Computer Theft," *eWeek*, August 10, 2006, at [http://www.eweek.com/article2/0,1895,2002148,00.asp?kc=EWNAVEMNL081106EOAD].
U.S. Department of Education - exposed loan data	August 2006	students who borrowed money under the Federal Direct Student Loan program	21,000	names, birth dates, SSNs, addresses, phone numbers and in some cases account information for holders of federal direct student loans	Yen, Hope, "Ed. Dept. offers free credit monitoring," *Houston Chronicle*, August 24, 2006 (no page given).
Naval Safety Center - personal data exposed on website and on 1,100 computer discs mailed to naval commands	July 2006	Naval and Marine Corps aviators and air crew, both active and reserve	"more than 100,000"	SSNs, personal information	"Naval Safety Center Finds Personal Data on Website," U.S. Department of Defense press release, July 8, 2006, at [http://www.news.navy.mil/search/display.asp?s tory_id=24568].

Table 4. Continued

Government (Local, State and Federal) Incidents	Date Publicized	Who Was Affected	Number Affected	Type of Data Released/Compromised	Source(s)
U.S. State Department - hackers	July 2006	Washington headquarters, and the Bureau of East Asian and Pacific Affairs	unknown	access to data and passwords	"State Department Releases Details Of Computer System Attacks," *COMMWEB*, July 13, 2006 (no page given), and Greenemeier, Larry, "State Department Hack Escalates Federal Data Insecurity," Information Week, July 12, 2006, at [http://www.informationweek.com/news/showArticle.jhtml?articleID=190302905].
Minnesota Department of Revenue (St. Paul, MN) - missing data tape	June 2006	individuals and businesses (taxpayers)	2,400 individuals and 48,000 businesses	names, addresses, SSNs, employment data	MN Department of Revenue, "Department of Revenue to Assist Taxpayers Whose Private Information Was Included in a Package Lost in the Mail," June 28, 2006, at [http://www.taxes.state.mn.us/taxes/publications/press_releases/content/taxpayer_information.sh tml]
Department of Energy- file stolen by hacker	June 2006	employees of the Energy Department's nuclear weapons agency	1,500	names, SSNs, birth datess, codes showing where the employees worked, codes showing their security clearance	*Associated Press*, "DOE Computers Hacked; Info on 1,500 Taken," June 11, 2006.

Table 4. Continued

Government (Local, State and Federal) Incidents	Date Publicized	Who Was Affected	Number Affected	Type of Data Released/Compromised	Source(s)
Government Accountability Office (GAO) - website exposed data from audit reports on Defense Department travel vouchers from the 1970s	June 2006	DoD employees	"fewer than 1,000"	service members' names, SSNs, addresses	Thormeyer, Rob, "GAO Removes Archived Personal Data from Web Site," WashingtonTechnology.com, June 27, 2006 at [http://www.washingtontechnology.com/news/1_1/daily_news/28845-1.html].
King County Records, Elections, and Licensing Services Division (Seattle, WA) - website exposed personal data	June 2006	current and former county residents	unknown (potentially thousands)	SSNs	*Associated Press*, "Councilman Irked by Data Postings on Web," June 27, 2006.
Internal Revenue Service - lost laptop	June 2006	IRS employees and job applicants	291	names, birth dates, SSNs, fingerprints	Lee, Christopher, "IRS Laptop Lost with Data on 291 People," *Washington Post*, June 8, 2006, p. A4.
Nebraska Treasurer's Office (Lincoln, NE) - hacker broke into a child-support computer system	June 2006	individuals and employers who pay and receive child support payments	300,000 individuals and 9,000 employers	names, SSNs, tax identification numbers for businesses	Nebraska State Treasurer, "Hacker Virus Stopped by Treasurer's Office," June 29, 2006, at [http://www.treasurer.state.ne.us/ie/server.asp]

Table 4. Continued

Government (Local, State and Federal) Incidents	Date Publicized	Who Was Affected	Number Affected	Type of Data Released/Compromised	Source(s)
Pentagon, Tricare Management Activity - hackers break into server	May 2006	Defense Department conference attendees	14,000	names, SSNs, credit card numbers, employer identification, other personal information	Barr, Stephen, "Conference Attendees' Personal Data May Be at Risk," *Washington Post*, May 12, 2006, p. D4.
Department of Veterans Affairs - laptop and external hard drive stolen	May 2006	military veterans	26.5 million	names, birth dates, SSNs	Lee, Christopher and Steve Vogel, "Personal Data on Veterans is Stolen," *Washington Post*, May 23, 2006, p. A1.
National Institutes of Health (NIH) - posting of confidential grant applications	October 2005	applicants to the NIH	undisclosed	grant proposals and other grant review materials	Pulley, John L., "NIH Accidentally Posts Confidential Grant Applications on the Web," *The Chronicle of Higher Education*, October 31, 2005 (no page given).
U.S. Air Force - records stolen from the Air Force Personnel Center's online Assignment Management System	August 2005	officers and 19 NCOs	33,300	SSNs, birth dates, and other sensitive information	Dorsett, Amy, "Identity theft Threat Hangs over AF Officers," *San Antonio Express-News*, August 24, 2005, p. 1A.
San Diego County Employees Retirement Association - hackers broke into two computers	July 2005	current and retired county government employees	33,000	workers' names, Social Security numbers, addresses and dates of birth	Chacon, Daniel, "Hackers Breach County's Personal Records; 33,000 People at Risk in Retirement Association," *San Diego Union-Tribune*, July 30, 2005, p. B1.

Table 4. Continued

Government (Local, State and Federal) Incidents	Date Publicized	Who Was Affected	Number Affected	Type of Data Released/Compromised	Source(s)
Federal Deposit Insurance Corporation - computer breach in early 2004. The agency wrote to employees that it learned of the breach only "recently", but did not explain how the breach occurred, aside from stating that it was not the result of a computer security failure.	June 2005	FDIC current and former employees or anyone employed at the agency as of July 2002.	6,000	names, birth dates, SSNs, and salary information	Krim, Jonathan, "FDIC Alerts Employees of Data Breach", *Washington Post*, June 16 2005, p. D1.
Lucas County (OH) Children Services - information from the agency's personnel database was compiled and e-mailed to an outside computer	June 2005	agency's 400 current employees and about 500 others who have worked there since 1991	900	names, telephone numbers, SSNs	Patch, David, "Lucas County Children Services Data Stolen," *Toledo Blade*, June 28, 2005, p. B1.
hackers breached Illinois Employment Development Department server	February 2004	people who work as domestic employees and those who employ them	90,000	SSNs, wages	"Hackers Breach State Files on 90,000," *Chicago Tribune*, February 15, 2004, p. 12.

Table 4. Continued

Government (Local, State and Federal) Incidents	Date Publicized	Who Was Affected	Number Affected	Type of Data Released/Compromised	Source(s)
U.S. Department of Defense - hackers downloaded Navy credit cards	August 2003	Navy's purchase card program, used to order routine office supplies	13,000	credit card numbers	Reddy, Anitha, "Hackers Steal 13,000 Credit Card Numbers; Navy Says No Fraud Has Been Noticed," *Washington Post*, November 23, 2003, p. E1.
Bronx identity theft ring filed thousands of fraudulent income tax returns	February 2003	income tax filers	not specified	SSNs **note:** ID theft ring obtained $7million in tax refunds	Weiser, Benjamin, "19 Charged in Identity Theft That Netted $7 Million in Tax Refunds," *New York Times*, February 5, 2003, p. B3.

Table 5. Data Security Breaches in Health Care (2003-2007)

Healthcare Incidents	Date Publicized	Who Was Affected	Number Affected	Type of Data Released/Compromised	Source(s)
Georgia Dept. of Community Health (Atlanta, GA) and private contractor Affiliated Computer Services (ACS) - missing computer disk	April 2007	state health care recipients	2,900,000	SSNs, addresses, birthdates, dates of eligibility, full names, Medicaid or children's health care recipient identification numbers	Miller, Andy, and Bill Hendrick, "Georgians' personal data lost; Medicaid, PeachCare clients: A computer disk including Social Security numbers on 2.9 million people was lost in transit," *Atlanta Journal and Constitution*, April 11, 2007, p. 1A.
DCH Health Systems (Tuscaloosa, AL) - lost computer disk and documents	April 2007	employees and retirees	6,000	retirement benefit information, SSNs, other uspecified personal information	Associated Press State & Local Wire, "Tuscaloosa-based DCH loses personal data on employees," April 5, 2007.
Group Health Cooperative Health Care System (Seattle, WA) - two laptops missing	March 2007	patients and employees	31,000	names, addresses, SSNs, group health numbers	"Pacific Northwest," *Seattle Times*, March 27, 2007, p. B3.
Westerly Hospital (Westerly, RI) - patients' confidential information posted on public website	March 2007	patients	2,242	names, SSNs, insurance information	Armental, Maria, "Data breach at Westerly Hospital," *Providence Journal* (Rhode Island), March 2, 2007.

Table 5. Continued

Healthcare Incidents	Date Publicized	Who Was Affected	Number Affected	Type of Data Released/Compromised	Source(s)
Wellpoint, Inc (IN-based health insurer) - lost compact disk **Note:** Company found the CD less than a week later. WellPoint did not release any information on where the disk was found.	March 2007	members of its Empire Blue Cross and Blue Shield unit in New York	75,000	names, SSNs, health plan identification numbers, descriptions of medical services back to 2003	Freudenheim, Milt, "Medical Data on Empire Blue Cross Members May Be Lost," *New York Times*, March 14, 2007, and Gaudin, Sharon, "WellPoint Finds Missing CD With Data On 75,000 People," *Information Week*, March 15, 2007, at [http://www.informationweek.com/story/showArticle.jhtml?articleID=198001105&cid=RSSfeed_IWK_News].
Seton Family of Hospitals (Austin, TX) - stolen laptop	February 2007	patients who sought care as part of an outpatient or clinic visit since July 1, 2005	7,800	SSNs, dates of birth, insurance program numbers	Gaudin, Sharon, "Hospital Laptop Stolen; Info On 7,800 Patients At Risk," *Information Week*, February 26, 2007, at [http://www.informationweek.com/story/showArticle.jhtml?articleID=197008711&cid=RSSfeed_IWK_News].

Table 5. Continued

Healthcare Incidents	Date Publicized	Who Was Affected	Number Affected	Type of Data Released/Compromised	Source(s)
Johns Hopkins University (JHU) and Johns Hopkins Hospital (Baltimore, MD) - eight backup tapes containing personal information on JHU employees lost; one backup tape containing information on JH hospital patients lost	February 2007	new Johns Hopkins Hospital patients first seen between July 4 and Dec. 18, 2006	52,000 university employees and 83,000 hospital patients	information on the university payroll tapes included Social Security numbers and, in some cases, bank account information for present and former employees; information on hospital patients included names and dates of birth	Johns Hopkins Institutions press release, "Identity Alert: A Joint Statement from The Johns Hopkins University and The Johns Hopkins Hospital," February 7, 2007, at [http://www.jhu.edu/identityalert/releases/statement.html].
Gulf Coast Medical Center (Nashville, TN & Tallahassee, FL) - two computers missing in two separate incidents	February 2007	patients, employees and former employees	1,900 individuals were affected by a theft in Nashville, TN in November and 8,000 when another computer was stolen in Tallahassee	names, SSNs	Vavala, Donna, "Laptop thefts cause alarm: Devices contained hospital patient, employee information; no ID thefts reported," *News Herald* (Panama City, Florida), March 1, 2007.

Table 5. Continued

Healthcare Incidents	Date Publicized	Who Was Affected	Number Affected	Type of Data Released/Compromised	Source(s)
St. Mary's Hospital (Leonardtown, MD) - stolen laptop	February 2007	former and current hospital patients	130,000	names, SSNs, dates of birth	O'Brien, Dennis, " Second Hospital Reports Lost Data. St. Mary's Notifies 130,000, Days after Hopkins' Notice; Second Md. Hospital Reports Loss of Patients' Data," *Baltimore Sun*, February 13, 2007, p. A1.
Wellpoint/Anthem Blue Cross Blue Shield - cassette tapes stolen from a lock box held by vendor Concentra Preferred Systems	February 2007	Anthem members in Kentucky, Indiana, Ohio and Virginia	196,000	names, SSNs	Howington, Patrick, "Cassette tapes containing customer information were stolen from a lock box held by one of its vendors,"*Courier-Journal* (Louisville, Kentucky), February 15, 2007.
Ohio Board of Nursing - website posted names and SSNs of nurses twice in one month	January 2007	newly licensed nurses	3,031	names, SSNs	Hoholik, Suzanne, "Error puts nurses' personal data online," *Columbus Dispatch (OH)*, January 25, 2007.
Swedish Medical Center, Ballard Campus (Seattle, WA) - employee used patients' personal information to open credit card accounts	October 2006	patients	1,100	names, dates of birth, SSNs	Song, Kyung, "3 Swedish patients say IDs stolen at Ballard campus; worker fired; Employee allegedly opened credit cards; Hospital warns patients to watch for activity on their credit reports," *Seattle Times*, October 25, 2006, p. B4.

Table 5. Continued

Healthcare Incidents	Date Publicized	Who Was Affected	Number Affected	Type of Data Released/Compromised	Source(s)
Sisters of St. Francis Health Services via Advanced Receivables Strategy (Indianapolis, IN) - contractor inadvertently left CDs containing confidential billing information in a new computer bag she purchased but later returned to a store	October 2006	patients, employees, physicians and Board members	260,000 patients and 6,200 employees	names, SSNs	Lee, Daniel, "Lost and found: info on 260,000 patients," *Indianapolis Star*, October 25, 2006.
Erlanger Health System (Chattanooga, TN) - missing data device	September 2006	current and former employees	4,150	names, SSNs	Berry, Emily, "Erlanger loses computer device, personnel data," *Chattanooga Times/Free Press*, September 24, 2006.
Medco Health Solutions- stolen laptop	March 2006	Ohio state employees and their dependents	4,600	SSNs, birth dates	Weiss, Todd R., "Vendor Waited Six Weeks to Notify Ohio Officials of Data Breach," Computerworld, March 1, 2006, at [http://www.computerworld.com/printthis/2006/0,4814,109116,00.htm].

Table 5. Continued

Healthcare Incidents	Date Publicized	Who Was Affected	Number Affected	Type of Data Released/Compromised	Source(s)
Children's Health Council, San Jose, California - stolen backup tape	September 2005	patients, employees, and parents of patients	5,000-6,000	psychiatric records, evaluations and SSNs; also payroll data on hundreds of current and former employees and credit card information from parents of patients	Walsh, Diana, "Data Stolen from Children's Psychiatric Center," *San Francisco Chronicle*, September 20, 2005, p. B8.
San Jose Medical Group Management - desktop computers stolen from locked administrative office	April 2005	former patients from last seven years	185,000	names, addresses, SSNs, confidential medical information	Weiss, Todd, "Update: Stolen Computers Contain Data on 185,000 Patients," *Computerworld*, April 8, 2005, at [http://www.computerworld.com/databasetopics/data/story/0,10801,100961,00.html].
TriWest Healthcare Alliance - theft of a database containing names and SSNs	December 2002	military personnel and their dependents	500,000	names, addresses, SSNs	Gorman, Tom, "Reward Offered in Huge Theft of Identity Data; Stolen Computers Had Names, Social Security Numbers of 500,000 Military Families," *Los Angeles Times*, January 1, 2003, p. 14.

Source: The tables were prepared by CRS from publicly available and news media sources.

Note: URLs are listed for exclusively online sources; other publications are identified by name and date.

FOR ADDITIONAL READING

CRS Report RS22374. *Data Security: Federal and State Laws*, by Gina Marie Stevens.
CRS Report RL33273. *Data Security: Federal Legislative Approaches*, by Gina Marie Stevens.
CRS Report RS22484. *Identity Theft Laws: State Penalties and Remedies and Pending Federal Bills*, by Tara Alexandra Rainson.
CRS Report RL33005. *Information Brokers: Federal and State Laws*, by Angie A. Welborn.
CRS Report RL33612. *Department of Veterans Affairs: Information Security and Information Technology Management Reorganization*, by Sidath Viranga Panangala.
CRS Report RL31919. *Remedies Available to Victims of Identity Theft*, by Gina Marie Stevens.
CRS Report RS22082. *Identity Theft: The Internet Connection* (archived), by Marcia S. Smith.

REFERENCES

[1] For additional information on legislative proposals introduced after the VA data theft (and in light of several ongoing information security and information technology management issues at the VA), see CRS Report RL33612, *Department of Veterans Affairs: Information Security and Information Technology Management Reorganization*, by Sidath Viranga Panangala.

[2] Graeme Newman and Megan McNally, *Identity Theft Literature Review*, National Criminal Justice Reference Service (NCJRS), 2005, at [http://www.ncjrs.gov/pdffiles1/nij/grants/ 210459.pdf].

[3] Ibid., p. v.

[4] Ibid., p. 14.

[5] Francois Paget. *Identity Theft*, McAfee Avert Labs, January 2007, at [http://www.mcafee.com/us/local_content/white_papers/wp_id_theft _en.pdf]. This report discusses recent high-profile examples of identity theft and how several countries define this type of fraud and its scope; examines both the criminals and their techniques to better understand how identity theft has evolved in recent years; and focuses on the victims and consequences of identity theft.

[6] Ibid., p. 3.

[7] California Department of Consumer Affairs, Office of Privacy Protection, *Notice of Security Breach - Civil Code Sections1798.29 and 1798.82 - 1798.84*, updated June 24, 2003, at [http://www.leginfo.ca.gov/cgi-bin/displaycode?section=civ&group =01001-02000&file=1798.25-1798.29], [http://www.leginfo.ca.gov/ cgi-bin/displaycode?section= civ&group=01001-02000&file=1798.8 0-1798.84], and *Recommend-ed Practices on Notification of Security*

	References
	Breach Involving Personal Information, October 10, 2003, at [http://www.privacy.ca.gov/ recommendations/secbreach.pdf].
[8]	See *State Security Breach Notification Laws*, National Conference of State Legislatures at [http://www.ncsl.org/programs/lis/cip/priv/breachlaws.htm]. As of January 9, 2007, the following states have enacted security breach notification laws: Arizona, Arkansas, California, Colorado, Connecticut, Delaware, Florida, Georgia, Hawaii, Idaho, Illinois, Indiana, Kansas, Louisiana, Maine, Michigan, Minnesota, Montana, Nebraska, Nevada, New Hampshire, New Jersey, New York, North Carolina, North Dakota, Ohio, Oklahoma, Pennsylvania, Rhode Island, Tennessee, Texas, Utah, Vermont, Washington, Wisconsin. See also: *State PIRG Summary of State Security Freeze and Security Breach Notification Laws*, U.S. Public Interest Research Group (USPIRG) at [http://www.pirg.org/consumer/ credit/statelaws.htm#breach]. See also CRS Report RS22374, *Data Security: Federal and State Laws*, by Gina Marie Stevens.
[9]	A security freeze law allows a customer to block unauthorized third parties from obtaining his or her credit report or score. A consumer who places a security freeze on his or her credit report or score receives a personal identification number to gain access to credit information or to authorize the dissemination of credit information. See CRS Report RS22484, *Identity Theft Laws: State Penalties and Remedies and Pending Federal Bills*, Tara Alexandra Rainson.
[10]	Peter Katel, "Identity Theft: Can Congress Give Americans Better Protection?," *CQ Researcher*, June 10, 2005.
[11]	Kevin Poulsen, "Data Spills: 100 Million Served," *27B Stroke 6*, December 14, 2006, at [http://blog.wired.com/27bstroke6/2006/12/data_spills_100.html].
[12]	Tom Zeller, "An Ominous Milestone: 100 Million Data Leaks," *New York Times*, December 18, 2006, p. C3.
[13]	Identity Theft and Assumption Deterrence Act, as amended by P.L. 105-318, 112 Stat. 3007 (October 30, 1998), at [http://www.ftc.gov/os/statutes/itada/itadact.htm].
[14]	For an overview of the federal laws that could assist victims of identity theft with purging inaccurate information from their credit records and removing unauthorized charges from credit accounts, as well as federal laws that impose criminal penalties on those who assume another person's identity through the use of fraudulent identification documents, see CRS Report RL31919, *Remedies*

References

Available to Victims of Identity Theft, by Gina Marie Stevens. (Relevant state laws are also discussed.)

[15] Federal Trade Commission press release, "FTC Issues Annual List of Top Consumer Complaints," February 7, 2007, at [http://www.ftc.gov/ opa/2007/02/topcomplaints.htm].

[16] For a brief discussion of federal and state data security laws, see CRS Report RS22374, *Data Security: Federal and State Laws*, by Gina Marie Stevens.

[17] Privacy Rights Clearinghouse, *A Chronology of Data Breaches* at [http://www.privacyrights.org/ar/ChronDataBreaches.htm]. The Privacy Rights Clearinghouse (PRC) is a nonprofit consumer organization which seeks to raise consumers' awareness of how technology affects personal privacy, and to document privacy complaints. The chronology "begins with ChoicePoint's 2/15/05 announcement of its data breaches because it was a watershed event in terms of disclosure to the affected individuals."

[18] Phishing is an e-mail fraud method in which the perpetrator sends out legitimate-looking email in an attempt to gather personal and financial information from recipients. Typically, the messages appear to come from well-known and trustworthy websites. Websites that are frequently spoofed by phishers include PayPal, eBay, MSN, Yahoo, BestBuy, and America Online. (Source: SearchSecurity.com(powered by whatis.com), at [http://searchsecurity.techtarget.com/sDefinition/ 0,290660,sid14_gci916037,00.html].

[19] US-CERT, *Quarterly Trends and Analysis Report*, March 1, 2007, at [http://www.us-cert.gov/press_room/trendsandanalysisQ107.pdf]. This report summarizes and provides analysis of incident reports submitted to US-CERT during the first quarter of FY2007 (October 1, 2006, to December 31, 2006).

[20] Government Accountability Office, *Information Security: Persistent Weaknesses Highlight Need for Further Improvement*, GAO-07-751T, April 19, 2007, at [http://www.gao.gov/new.items/d07751t.pdf].

[21] Ibid., p.2.

[22] U.S. Department of Justice, Office of the Inspector General, Audit Division, *The Federal Bureau of Investigation's Control over Weapons and Laptop Computers Follow-up Audit, Audit Report 07-18*, February 2007, at [http://www.usdoj.gov/oig/reports/FBI/a0718/ final.pdf].

References

[23] Ibid., p. 6.
[24] Rebecca Adams, "Data Drip: How the Feds Handle Personal Data," *CQ Weekly*, July 10, 2006, p. 1846.
[25] Office of Management and Budget, *FY 2006 Report to Congress on Implementation of The Federal Information Security Management Act of 2002*, March 1, 2007 at [http://www.whitehouse.gov/omb/inforeg/ reports/2006_fisma_report.pdf].
[26] Zachary Goldfarb, "To Agency Insiders, Cyber Thefts And Slow Response Are No Surprise," *Washington Post*, July 18, 2006, at [http://www.washingtonpost.com/wp-dyn/content/article/2006/07/17/ AR2006071701170.html].
[27] In the 110th Congress, the House Government Reform Committee was renamed the House Committee on Oversight and Government Reform.
[28] U.S. House of Representatives. Committee on Government Reform, *Staff Report Agency Data Breaches since January 1, 2003* at [http://oversight.house.gov/story.asp?ID=1127]. See also Agency response letters at House Committee on Government Reform website at [http://oversight.house.gov/story.asp?ID=1127].
[29] Office of Management and Budget Memorandum for the Heads of Departments and Agencies, *Protection of Sensitive Agency Information*, June 23, 2006, at [http://www.whitehouse.gov/OMB/memoranda/ fy2006/m06-16.pdf].
[30] Ibid.
[31] Identity Theft Task Force website at [http://www.usdoj.gov/ittf/].
[32] Executive Order 13402, "Strengthening Federal Efforts to Protect Against Identity Theft," May 10, 2006, at [http://www.whitehouse.gov/ news/releases/2006/05/20060510-3.html].
[33] The President's Identity Theft Task Force, *Combating Identity Theft: A Strategic Plan*, April 2007 at [http://www.identitytheft.gov/reports/ StrategicPlan.pdf].
[34] Ibid.
[35] Center for Identity Management and Information Protection, at [http://www.utica.edu/ academic/institutes/cimip/].
[36] Dan Carnevale, "Why Can't Colleges Hold On to Their Data?," *Chronicle of Higher Education*, May 6, 2005, p. A35.

[37] Reuters, "U.S. Colleges Struggle to Combat Identity Theft," *eWeek*, August 17, 2005, at [http://www.findarticles.com/p/articles/mi_zdewk/is_200508/ai_n14906864].

[38] Andrea L. Foster, "Louisiana State U. Signs Deal to Protect Students and Employees in Case of Data Breach," *Chronicle of Higher Education*, September 13, 2006, at [http://chronicle.com/daily/2006/09/ 2006091301t.htm].

[39] AARP, "Into the Breach: Security Breaches and Identity Theft," July 2006, at [http://www.aarp.org/research/frauds-scams/fraud/dd142_security_breach.html].

INDEX

A

access, 9, 10, 14, 24, 25, 27, 33, 43, 46, 49, 50, 57, 59, 60, 72, 74, 88
accident victims, 65
accounting, 8, 49
administrators, 43
ADP, 18
age, 3
air traffic, 69, 70
Alabama, 64
America Online, 30, 89
Arizona, 30, 41, 88
arrest, 4
assets, 34
AT&T, 18
Athens, 38, 40
ATM, 62
attachment, 30
attacks, 3, 10
authentication, 10
awareness, 1, 4, 11, 89

B

Bank of America, 56, 58, 59, 60, 61
banking, 23
banks, 13, 27, 56, 60
benefits, 23

birth, 3, 7, 17, 18, 19, 23, 25, 28, 32, 34, 35, 36, 42, 44, 45, 46, 49, 50, 51, 53, 55, 57, 62, 63, 64, 65, 67, 71, 72, 73, 74, 75, 76, 77, 80, 81, 82, 83
black market, 4
blog, 88
blood, 51
Boeing, 17, 23
BP, 68
breaches, vii, 1, 3, 4, 5, 7, 8, 9, 11, 13, 14, 89
Breast, 66
breeding, 4
Britain, 30

C

California, 1, 4, 25, 32, 33, 36, 38, 43, 45, 46, 49, 50, 51, 52, 53, 59, 62, 64, 68, 84, 87, 88
Canada, 16, 30
cardiology, 53
CBO, 68, 69
CD, 21, 30, 68, 80
cell, 29
Census, 63, 71
Census Bureau, 63, 71
Chicago, 24, 27, 29, 30, 33, 37, 39, 65, 77
child welfare, 63

children, 79
classification, 44
clients, 27, 55, 58, 61, 64, 79
CNN, 22, 60
codes, 27, 59, 64, 74
colleges, 13, 70
community, 8, 15, 70
compensation, 19, 65
computer systems, 3, 10, 14, 16
computer use, 33
computers, 3, 9, 10, 14, 25, 26, 34, 36, 37, 38, 39, 43, 45, 46, 48, 59, 61, 66, 76, 81, 84
computing, 7
configuration, 9
Congress, 1, 9, 11, 88, 90
Congressional Budget Office, 68, 69
Connecticut, 46, 65, 88
Constitution, 42, 57, 79
consumers, 1, 5, 8, 11, 19, 25, 57, 89
corporations, 8, 11
crack, 46
credit, 1, 3, 4, 5, 7, 13, 15, 16, 18, 20, 21, 22, 24, 25, 26, 27, 28, 29, 30, 38, 39, 41, 44, 46, 48, 52, 54, 55, 57, 58, 59, 60, 61, 62, 63, 65, 72, 73, 76, 78, 82, 84, 88
credit card fraud, 3, 4
credit rating, 7
crime, 3, 4
criminals, 25, 55, 60, 87
CRS, 1, 7, 11, 12, 84, 85, 87, 88, 89
CT, 18
culture, 13
customers, 15, 16, 18, 20, 21, 22, 24, 25, 26, 27, 28, 29, 30, 31, 39, 54, 55, 56, 57, 58, 59, 60, 61, 62
cybercrime, 21, 60
cybersecurity, 8

D

danger, 3

database, 10, 21, 24, 25, 33, 40, 44, 49, 52, 67, 77, 84
definition, 3, 4
Democrat, 23
Department of Agriculture, 63
Department of Commerce, 71
Department of Defense, 72, 73, 78
Department of Energy, 74
Department of Homeland Security, 10
Department of Justice, 8, 89
disclosure, 89
discs, 65, 72, 73
District of Columbia, 55
doctors, 64
donors, 19, 20, 34, 41, 51
DSL, 18

E

East Asia, 72, 74
e-commerce, 30
education, 13
Education, 10, 13, 32, 33, 34, 35, 36, 37, 38, 39, 40, 41, 42, 43, 44, 45, 46, 47, 48, 49, 50, 51, 52, 53, 72, 73, 76, 90, 91
educational institutions, 14
email, 52, 68, 69, 89
employees, 10, 17, 18, 20, 21, 22, 23, 24, 25, 33, 34, 35, 36, 37, 38, 39, 42, 47, 48, 52, 55, 56, 60, 61, 64, 65, 67, 68, 69, 70, 74, 75, 76, 77, 79, 81, 83, 84
employment, 8, 74
environment, 13
equating, 7
equipment, 8, 13, 14, 18, 34, 66
equity, 58
evidence, 3
Executive Order, 10, 90
Exposure, 63

Index

F

FAA, 28, 69, 70
failure, 77
FBI, 9, 25, 48, 89
FDIC, 77
Federal Bureau of Investigation, 9, 89
federal government, 10, 27
federal law, 88
financial institutions, 13, 57, 62
firms, 1, 11, 58, 60
Ford, 22
fraud, 3, 4, 8, 11, 28, 47, 48, 87, 91
fuel, 22
funds, 19

G

garbage, 66
General Electric, 18
General Motors, 60
Georgia, 33, 42, 52, 63, 79, 88
government, 3, 8, 9, 10, 11, 13, 48, 55, 58, 76
Government Accountability Office (GAO), 9, 10, 75, 89
grades, 32, 37, 43
graduate students, 48, 50
grants, 87
guidelines, 10
Gulf Coast, 81

H

hacking, 3, 10, 35, 43, 44, 45, 46
harvesting, 21
Hawaii, 47, 88
health, 4, 16, 19, 38, 70, 79, 80
health care, 79
health insurance, 16
Heart, 41
high school, 37, 67
higher education, 13
hospitals, 71
House, 10, 90
households, 71
human resources, 25

I

IBM, 27
id, 28, 41, 48, 72, 73, 87
Idaho, 34, 88
identification, 36, 44, 45, 75, 76, 79, 80, 88
identity, 3, 4, 7, 8, 11, 13, 36, 38, 47, 65, 66, 78, 87, 88
images, 41
Incidents, 15, 16, 17, 18, 19, 20, 21, 22, 23, 24, 25, 26, 27, 28, 29, 30, 31, 32, 33, 34, 35, 36, 37, 38, 39, 40, 41, 42, 43, 44, 45, 46, 47, 48, 49, 50, 51, 52, 53, 54, 55, 56, 57, 58, 59, 60, 61, 62, 63, 64, 65, 66, 67, 68, 69, 70, 71, 72, 73, 74, 75, 76, 77, 78, 79, 80, 81, 82, 83, 84
income, 78
income tax, 78
indication, 67
industry, 8
information sharing, 11
information technology, 87
inspectors, 9
institutions, 13, 14
insurance, 4, 13, 19, 20, 37, 47, 70, 71, 79, 80
intellectual property, 40
Internal Revenue Service, 10, 66, 75
Internet, 3, 4, 12, 14, 26, 29, 32, 42, 43, 57, 61, 85
intrusions, 9
investors, 18
Ireland, 16

J

Japan, 30, 58
journalism, 41

K

Kentucky, 40, 70, 82
King, 75

L

laptop, 3, 9, 10, 17, 18, 19, 20, 23, 24, 37, 40, 42, 44, 47, 50, 51, 54, 55, 56, 58, 59, 61, 63, 64, 67, 68, 71, 73, 75, 76, 80, 82, 83
law enforcement, 4, 11, 22
laws, 1, 5, 88, 89
legislation, 1, 5, 11
legislative proposals, 87
licenses, 4, 62
loans, 34, 61, 62, 63, 72, 73
local government, 8
Los Angeles, 31, 36, 51, 53, 61, 64, 84
Louisiana, 13, 88, 91
luggage, 18

M

mail fraud, 89
Maine, 88
malware, 8
management, 9, 11, 87
marketing, 27
Massachusetts, 65
measures, 1, 10, 11
media, 84
Medicaid, 79
Medicare, 64
membership, 34
merchandise, 16
messages, 89

Mexico, 64
Miami, 43, 57
Microsoft, 27
military, 76, 84
Minnesota, 37, 54, 74, 88
Mississippi, 35
Missouri, 33
money, 22, 30, 60, 72, 73
Montana, 34, 88
Moscow, 34
mothers, 62
motivation, 4
music, 30

N

nation, 1, 4
National Guard, 64
National Institutes of Health, 10, 76
Nebraska, 75, 88
network, 8, 26, 36, 46, 48, 49
New Jersey, 60, 88
New Mexico, 32
New York, 7, 17, 18, 19, 23, 28, 56, 59, 66, 67, 78, 80, 88
New York Times, 7, 23, 56, 59, 78, 80, 88
Newton, 40
NIH, 76
North Carolina, 60, 71, 88
Notre Dame, 41
nuclear weapons, 74
nurses, 82

O

Office of Management and Budget, 10, 90
Oklahoma, 37, 88
OMB, 10, 90
organization(s), 8, 40, 89
orientation, 35
oversight, 90

Index

P

Pacific, 20, 31, 68, 72, 74, 79
Panama, 81
parents, 63, 84
password, 10, 13, 18, 54
patents, 40
payroll, 23, 63, 64, 81, 84
penalties, 88
Pentagon, 76
personal, 1, 3, 5, 7, 9, 10, 11, 14, 20, 21, 25, 32, 33, 34, 35, 36, 37, 39, 40, 41, 44, 45, 48, 49, 51, 53, 54, 55, 56, 57, 58, 61, 64, 65, 66, 68, 69, 70, 71, 72, 73, 75, 76, 79, 81, 82, 88, 89
personal computers, 3
photographs, 45, 53
police, 16, 17, 34, 66, 67
prices, 55
privacy, 8, 25, 27, 49, 88, 89
private sector, 11
profit, 55, 63
program, 48, 51, 52, 61, 63, 72, 73, 78
programming, 27
public sector, 11
Puerto Rico, 16

Q

questioning, 18

R

Red Cross, 19
regional, 19, 69, 70
rehabilitation, 53
retail, 27
retirees, 55, 79
retirement, 79
returns, 4, 78
Rhode Island, 79, 88
risk, 9, 11, 15, 18, 34, 36, 63, 64, 67
routing, 25, 57, 58, 63

S

sales, 15
school, 32, 34, 37, 38, 39, 40, 41, 43, 48, 49, 70
search, 72, 73
Secretary of State, 63
securities, 13, 19, 60
security, 1, 3, 4, 5, 8, 9, 10, 11, 13, 14, 16, 19, 21, 22, 28, 35, 48, 49, 52, 54, 58, 59, 60, 67, 68, 74, 77, 87, 88, 89, 91
September 11, 30
series, 1, 10, 11
SEVIS, 49, 53
shares, 18, 55
sharing, 34
Silicon Valley, 21
sites, 10, 14, 29
skimming, 22
Social Security, 1, 3, 4, 7, 8, 11, 14, 23, 37, 40, 42, 45, 47, 56, 63, 65, 69, 70, 76, 79, 81, 84
social workers, 66
software, 9, 16, 41, 56, 66
South Carolina, 36
Spain, 37
St. Louis, 54
stages, 3
standards, 11
State Department, 10, 66, 72, 74
state laws, 89
statistics, 8
statutes, 88
stock, 21, 57
storage, 23
Student and Exchange Visitor Information System, 49, 53
students, 13, 32, 33, 34, 35, 36, 37, 39, 40, 41, 42, 43, 44, 45, 46, 47, 48, 49, 50, 51, 52, 53, 67, 72, 73
subscribers, 19, 27, 31, 68, 69
suffering, 14
summer, 44

Sun, 27, 29, 30, 35, 39, 63, 82
supervisors, 36
suspects, 66
systems, 39

T

takeover, 4
targets, 13
taxpayers, 66, 74
technology, 60, 89
teens, 30
telemarketing, 4
telephone, 36, 44, 77
Tennessee, 39, 42, 88
terminals, 26
test scores, 40
Texas, 36, 37, 41, 44, 52, 67, 88
Thailand, 30
theft, 3, 4, 7, 8, 11, 13, 14, 15, 17, 18, 21, 22, 23, 32, 34, 36, 38, 40, 42, 47, 51, 56, 58, 63, 64, 65, 66, 67, 76, 78, 81, 84, 87, 88
threat(s), 7, 8
time, 4, 29, 47
Time Warner, 23
trade, 27
transactions, 16, 26, 55, 58
Transportation Security Administration, 63
trend, 4
TSA, 63

U

UK, 16

United States, 8, 30
universities, 1, 11
USDA, 63
users, 8, 58
Utah, 88

V

Vermont, 88
veterans, 3, 64, 67, 76
victimization, 4
victims, 7, 8, 55, 66, 87, 88
Virginia, 35, 50, 64, 67, 82
visas, 4
voters, 63, 65
vouchers, 75

W

wages, 77
Wall Street Journal, 20, 24, 25, 30, 61
Washington, 22, 24, 39, 53, 55, 56, 58, 59, 63, 71, 72, 74, 75, 76, 77, 78, 88, 90
watershed, 89
websites, 3, 30, 89
wholesale, 4
Wisconsin, 88
women, 66
workers, 10, 19, 23, 45, 55, 65, 76
workstation, 68, 69
World Economic Forum, 29